Writings in Connection with
the Donatist Controversy –
Introductory Essay

Writings in Connection with the Donatist Controversy – Introductory Essay

St. Augustine

Writings in Connection with the Donatist Controversy – Introductory Essay

© Lighthouse Publishing 2018

Written by: St. Augustine (Nov.13 354 – Aug.28 430)
Translated by: Rev. J.R. King M.A
Revised with additional notes by: Rev. Chester D. Hartranft, D.D.
Updated into Modern U.S English by A.M. Overett (b. 1960)

All rights reserved. Without limiting the rights under copyright reserved above, no part of this publication may be reproduced, stored in a retrieval system, or transmitted, in any form or by any means (electronic, mechanical, photocopying, recording or otherwise), without the prior written permission of the copyright owner of this book.

Published by
Lighthouse Christian Publishing
SAN 257-4330
5531 Dufferin Drive
Savage, Minnesota, 55378
United States of America

www.lighthousechristianpublishing.com

Chapter I.—Bibliography.

A. Sources.

I. Of course all the Anti-Donatist writings of Augustin are found in the general editions from Amerbach, 1506, to Migne, 1861. A few are also collected in Du Pin's edd. of Optatus Mil. 1. In the Monumenta vetera ad Donatistarum Historiam pertinentia. 2. In the Gesta Collationis Carthagini habitae Honorii Caesaris iussu inter Catholicos et Donatistas. See also the different Collections of Councils, Labbe, Baluze, Harduin, Mansi, etc. Since these works are discussed in Chapter II. it is unnecessary to repeat the titles here. Cp. titles in Retractationes: and Indiculus librorum, tractatuum et epistolarum S. Augustini, ed. cura Possidii, cap. III.

II. Separate editions of Augustin's Anti-Donatist writings. (From Schönemann's Bibliotheca, and other bibliographies.)

1. S. Augustini liber seu Epistola de unitate Ecclesiae contra Petiliani Donat. Epistolam, Argumentis, Notis atque Analysi illustrata, studio Justi Caluini. Moguntiae. 1602.

2. SS. Cypriani et Augustini de unitate Ecclesiae tractatus. Accedit Georgii Calixti, S. Theo. Doct. et in Acad. Julia Prof. primarii, in eorundem librorum lectionem Introductionis fragmentum edente Frid. Ulrico Calixto. Georgii filio. Helmæstadii ex typogr. Calixt. 1657. 8.

3. Aurelii Augustini, Episcopi Hipponensis, Liber de Unitate Ecclesiae contra Donatistas. Ext. cum Commentariis uberrimis et utilissimis in Melchioris

Writings in Connection with the Donatist Controversy - Introductory Essay

Lydeckeri Historia illustrata Ecclesiae Africanae, cujus totum pæne tomum secundum constituit inscriptum: Tomus secundus ad Librum Augustini de Unitate Ecclesiae contra Donatistas, de principiis Ecclesiae Africanae, illiusque fide in Articulis de Capite Christo et Ecclesia, de Unitate et Schismate, plurimisque Religionis Christianae capitibus agit. Ultrajecti apud viduam Guil. Clerck, 1690. 4.

4. D. Augustini liber de moderate coercendis haereticis ed Bonifacium Comitem. Nic. Bergius Revalensis Holmiae, 1696, in8.

III. Translations.

1. Epistre ou le Livre de St. Augustin de l'Unité de l'Eglise, contre Petilien, Evesque Donatiste, avec certaines observations pour entendre les lieux plus difficiles par Jac. Tigeou, imprimé à Reims par Jean de Foigny. 1567. 8.
2. L'Epistre à Vincent, Evesque de l'heresie Rogatiane, traduict de latin par Clément Vaillant. A Paris, Mathurin Prevost. 1573. 8.
3. Traité du Baptême trad. par l'abbé Dujat, chapelain d'Étampes. Paris. 1778. 12.
4. Writings in connection with the Donatist controversy, translated by the Rev. J. R. King, M.A. In the Series of Translations of the Works of Augustin. Edinburgh. T. & T. Clark. 1872.
5. Ausgewählte Schriften des heil. Aurelius Augustinus, Kirchenlehrers, nach aem Urtexte ubersetzt. Mit einer kurzen Lebensbeschreibung des Heiligen von J. Motzberger. 1871–1879. In der Bibliothek der Kirchenväter, Kempten, 1869 sqq.

B. Literature.

This is a selected literature of the Donatist controversy so far as Augustin was connected with it. I. In the Benedictine editions occur:

    1.   Their Vita S. Aurelii Augustini. Tom. XI. Antw., pp. 1–344. Tom. I. Migne, pp. 65–578.
    2.   Praefatio of Tom. IX. Antw. s. p. Migne, pp. 9–24.
    3.   Index opusculorum S. Augustini contra Donatistas. Tom. IX. Antw., pp. 463, 4. Migne, pp. 757–760.
    4.   Excerpta et scripta vetera ad Donatistarum historiam pertinentia. Tom. IX. Antw., App. pp. 7–50. Migne, pp. 773–842.
    5.   Epistolarum ordo chronologicus. Tom. II. Antw., s. p. Migne, pp. 13–48.

    II.   Possidius: Vita S. Aurelii Augustini. Reprinted in Migne Aug. Op. Tom. I., pp. 33–66. Cp. Migne Pat. Lat. L. p. 407.
    III.   Ecclesiastica Historia. By the Magdeburg Centuriators. 1559–1574. Tom. II. and III., Centuria, IV. and V., contain the Donatist history.
    IV.   Balduinius, Franc.

    1.   Delibatio Africanae historiae ecclesticae, s. Optati libri VII. de Schismate Donatistarum, etc. Paris, 1563. A second edition with improved readings. Ib., 1569. In this the prefaces and annotations are of value. Reprinted in Du Pin's ed. of Optatus Mil.

2. Historia Carthaginensis Collationis sive disputationis de ecclesia, olim habitae inter Catholicos et Donatistas. Paris, 1566. 8. Reprinted in Du Pin. ib.
V. Baronius. Annales Ecclesiatici. 1588–1607. Tom. III.-V., contain the Donatist history.
VI. Albaspinæus: Optati Mel. opera cum notis et observationibus Gabrielis Albaspinæi. Paris, 1631. Valuable mainly for the observations; reprinted in Du Pin's ed. of Optatus.
VII. Casaubonus: Optati Mel. de schismate Donatistarum libri VII. In eosd. notae et emendationes Merici Casauboni. Lond. 1631. These notes are of value and are reproduced with those of other editions in the Annotationes Variorumof Du Pin's ed.
VIII. Valesius Henricus: Eusebii Pamph. Historia ecc., libri de Vita Constantini, Panegyricus, Const. Oratio ad Sanctorum coetum, gr. et lat. cum annotatt. Paris, 1659 and often. In this is his dissertation: De schismate Donatistarum.
IX. Long, Thomas, B.D. History of the Donatists. Lond. 1677. 8.
X. Du Pin: Nouvelle Bibliothéque des Auteurs Ecclésiastiques.
1. St. Augustin. Tom. III.première partie, pp. 522–839, 1690. Particularly the review of vol. IX. of Augustin's collected works, pp. 792–811.
2. In Tom. II.,Troisième partie, 1701, there are also many allusions to the history and literature.
3. In his ed. of Optatus Mel., Historia Donatistarum.

XI. Ittig, Thomas: de Haeresiarchis œvi apostolici at apostol. prox. Lips. 1690–1703. 4.

XII.	Leydecker Melchior; Historia Ecclesiastica Africana. 2 Tom. 4, See above. Traj. 1690. 4.
XIII.	Witsius, Hermann: Miscellaneorum Sacrorum libri. 2 vols. Amst. 1692. 4. In vol. I. Dissertatio de schismate Donatistarum.
XIV.	Bernino: Historia di tutte l'heresie descritta da Domenico Bernino. Venezia 1711. Tom. I., contains hist. of Donatism.
XV.	Storren, J. Ph.: ansführlicher und gründlicher Bericht von den Namen, Ursprung, v.s.w. der Donatisten. Frankf. 1723. 8.
XVI.	Norisius, Henricus: Opera omnia nunc prim. collecta et ordinata. Veronae, Tumermani, 1729–32, fol. 4vols. The fourth volume contains his posthumous work on History of Donatism, as finished by Ballerini.
XVII.	Tillemont: in his Memoires pour servir a l'histoire Ecclésiastique:
1.	Tom. VI. Histoire du schisme des Donatistes, où l'on marque aussi tout ce qui regardé l'Eglise d'Afrique depuis l'an305, jusques en l'an391que S. Augustin fut fait Prestre. 1732.
2.	Tom. XIII. La Vie de Saint Augustin, dans laquelle on trouvera l'histoire des Donatistes de son temps, et celle des Pelagiens. 1732.
XVIII.	Orsi: Della Istoria Ecclesiastica descritta da F. Guiseppe Agostino Orsi. Tom. IV. (1741) and V. (1749) contain the history of the Donatists.
XIX.	Walch, Ch. Wilh. Fr.: Entwurf einer vollständigen Historie der Ketzereien, Spaltungen und Religionsstreitigkeiten, bis auf die Zeiten der Reformation. Leipzig, 1768. Vierter Theil: Von der

Spaltung der Donatisten; with its three sections:
a. Von der historie der Donatisten.
b. Von den zwischen den Donatisten und ihren Gegnern geführten Religionsstreitigkeiten.
c. Beurtheilung der Donatistichen Streitigkeiten. This work was the beginning of a new critical estimate of the documents.

XX. Schröckh, Johann Mattheus: Christliche Kirchengeschichte. Sechster Theil: 1784, but particularly Elfter Theil, 1786. A juster estimate of Donatism.

XXI. Morcellii, Steph. Ant.: Africa christiana in tres partes distributa. 3 vols. 4Brixiae,1816–17. 4. P. II.for Donatism.

XXII. Bindemann, C.: Der heilige Augustinus, 1844–1869. Bdd. II. & III. contain excellent analyses of the works on Donatism, as well as a history during Augustin's life.

XXIII. Roux, Adrianus: Dissertatio de Aurelio Augustino, adversario Donatistarum. Lugduni Batavorum, 1838. A brief summary of the works and doctrine.

XXIV. Ribbeck: Donatus und Augustinus oder der erste entscheidende Kampf zwischen Separatismus und Kirche. Ein Kirchenhistorischer Versuch von Ferdinand Ribbeck. Elberfeld. 1857. 8. An uncritical history; but a vigorous analysis, apologetic and polemic.

XXV. Deutsch: Drei Actenstücke zur Geschichte Donatismus. Neu herausgegeben und erklärt von Martin Deutsch. Berlin, 1875. The first work on the textual and historical criticism of the sources.

XXVI. Voelter: Der Ursprung des

Donatismus, nach den Quellen untersucht und dargestellt von Lic Dr. Daniel Voelter. Freiburg i. B. und Tübingen, 1883. This keen writer, at present Prof. Ord. in Univ. of Amsterdam, has gone still further into textual and historical criticism, and gives fair promise of a more impartial hearing for Donatism. It is to be hoped that he will fulfill his qualified promise of further research. Among the general church histories particular mention may be made of Gieseler, Neander, Lindner, Niedner, Robertson, Ritter, Hergenröther, Schaff. The articles on Augustin, Donatism and related persons and topics in Ceillier, Ersch und Gruber, Herzog, Schaff-Herzog, Smith's Dictionary of Christian Biography, Wetzer and Welte, Lichtenberger, are more or less noteworthy. Mention must also be made of the Patrologies, the biographies, Hefele's Conciliengeschichte, the Analyses Patrum, etc.

Chapter II. —An Analysis of Augustin's Writings Against the Donatists.

The object of this chapter is to present a rudimentary outline and summary of all that Augustin penned or spoke against those traditional North African Christians whom he was pleased to regard as schismatics. It will be arranged, so far as may be, in chronological order, following the dates suggested by the Benedictine edition. The necessary brevity precludes anything but a very meagre treatment of so considerable a theme. The writer takes no responsibility for the ecclesiological tenets of the great Father, nor will he enter here into any criticism of the text and truth of the documents, upon which the historical argument was so laboriously and peremptorily built, to the utter ignoring of the Donatist archives, and the protests of their scholars against the validity and integrity of their opponents' records. Both parties claimed to be the historic Catholic church; both were little apart in doctrine, worship, and polity; both tended toward externalism in piety; both accused one another of fraud in inventing records. Later Romanism in its bright spirit of selection took much spoil from either camp.

    The city of Augustin's birth, its neighborhood, indeed the whole ecclesiastical province of Numidia, was a stronghold for this puristic school. Is it not singular, then, that it seems to have made no impression upon his early years? As a child he had witnessed its brief restoration under Julian, and then the severe or lax efforts at suppression under succeeding emperors; the Rogatian schism and the Tychonian reformation were quite familiar to him in his Manichæan period; but the Confessions are silent as to any such stamp or hold upon his mind. His activity begins with his ordination to the presbyterate, a time marked in Donatist annals by the Maximianist separation, and increases as he becomes bishop. From about 392 to near the close of his life, pen and voice were seldom still. In all those years the outlinear thoughts grew in breadth and depth; endless are the forms in which his few and radical conceptions manifest themselves; never does he lose sight of the popular effect, so that he knows when to relax his love of word-play and delight in mysterious inductions, in order to make the chief themes plain to the dullest mind.

    How varied the channels through which he struggled for the mastery of his idea of the Church! In the pulpit he made Donatism the occasion of many a polemic, many an appeal; in his correspondence it was an everrecurrent topic; it was the staple of many a tract and book; verse was not shunned to destroy its fashionableness and popularity; commentaries and manuals for the meditative hour or for the training of the theological student, abounded in warnings against its aggressiveness; no opportunity for debate or conference or epistolary discussion was left unimproved. And no wonder: it was a living thing, of the street, of the market, of the social circle, of the home; it threatened at times to obliterate the transmarine view of the church from North Africa; its spirit of political independence and plea for religious liberty went to the hearts of a people, more and more restive under the decline of the Empire.

The literary creations of Donatism had been somewhat more fertile than that of Cæcilianism. We must not belittle Donatus the Great, Parmenian, Petilian, Gaudentius, and certainly the eminence of Tychonius is confessed by Augustin himself. Up to this time Optatus of Milevis had been the only forcible opponent. But against the great Augustin whom could they bring into the field? And against the great Augustin, backed by the energy of the State, there was little hope of fairness. Augustin found a new and weighty school. Donatism, with its impossible ideal, already began to despise the culture which seemed to help its defeat and withdrew into its sensitive shell after the manner of all puristic tendencies under persecution.

The two prevalent lines of attack are the historical on the origin of the schism, which involved the dissection of the documents, and the doctrinal, or the discussion of the true notes of the Church from the basis of the Scriptures. This latter Augustin preferred, because final;

he bowed to no patristic. One or the other or both may be traced in all his works, great or small, against them. Out of so protracted a controversy there grew up a symmetrical and comprehensive theory of the Church and the Sacraments on either side.

Of three fundamental points of Donatism, as perpetuated practices of North Africa, rebaptism and the encouragement of a martyr spirit with its attendant feasts, the continuance of the Seniores in the government of the Church, we find Augustin aiming mainly at the overthrow of the first two. One of his earliest letters suggests to his bishop some means for checking the drunkenness and great excess connected with the Natalitia. Passing to the specific subject in view:

In the early period of his presbyterate, (possibly about 392, others place it later), Augustin journeyed through Mutugenna, which apparently belonged to his bishop's see. He learned how pacifically disposed Maximin, Donatist bishop of Sinaita, was. The friendly feeling thus kindled toward him was shaken by the rumor that he had rebaptized a defecting Catholic deacon of Mutugenna; not willing to credit the story, he visited the deacon's home. His parents testified to their son's reception into the same office by the Donatists. In the absence of Bishop Valerius, he writes to Maximin with entreaty, refusing to credit the repetition of the rite, and urging him to remain firm in the convictions which had been imputed to him. He solicits a reply, that both letters may be read in the public service, after the dismission of the military. The prominent points of the letter are: while declining to recognize the validity of Maximin's orders, he does not refuse to salute him as Dominus dulcissimus, and Pater venerabilis. His solicitude as a shepherd to do his duty to all the sheep, constrains him to force himself upon their attention, and to be eager for correspondence or conference with a view to bringing them back to the fold. He is perfectly assured of the absolute and final correctness of his idea of the Church, and of the hopeless error of Donatism, an error so great as to merit eternal destruction. He discriminates, however, between heresy and schism at this time. Rebaptism in any case is a sin, but as applied to apostatizing Catholics, is an immanissimum scelus. There is only one baptism; that of Christ; as there was no double circumcision, so the sacrament of the New Testament should not be repeated. The Church is the owner of the nations which are Christ's inheritance, and of the ends of the earth, which are his possession; hence it is universal; the seamless robe should not be rent. Moreover, the Lord's threshing-floor has chaff upon it along with the wheat, and therefore he urged the disuse of imputations through unworthy members on either side, whether Macarius or Circumcelliones. The schism made itself disastrously felt in all domestic and social relations. He engages to avoid anything that would look like using the power of the state for coercing conscience, and begs that on Maximin's side the Circumcelliones may be restrained. [Ep. xxiii.]

    A Plenary council of all Africa was convened in Hippo-Regius in 393, before which Augustin preached the sermon. His subject was Faith and the Creed: his handling made such an impression that he was induced to expand it into the treatise: De Fide et Symbolo. In explaining the article credimus et sanctam ecclesiam, utique catholicam, he reflects on heretics and schismatics as claiming the title of churches for their congregations; and distinguishes between these two opponents of the

Catholic body, heretics erring in doctrine, schismatics, while like the Catholic body in views of truth yet transgressing in the rupture of fraternal love. Neither pertain to the true Church of God. (Cp. Retractt. I. xvii).

Determined if possible to win the ear of all classes, the presbyter next affected a poem, "Psalmus contra Partem Donati," in the art of an Abecedarium, running the letters to U. The line with which it began was to be chanted as a refrain after each group of usually twelve lines connected with each letter, the whole closing with an extended epilogue. A generally vulgar performance it is, and purposely disclaimed all metrical dignity; and yet it contains the germs of his logical and historical opinions on the controverted points. The Church is a net in the sea of the world, enclosing the good and bad, which are not to be separated until the net is drawn to the shore. Those who accuse the Catholics of tradition, were themselves traditors and broke the net. The history is repeated, and all proof of the Donatist charges declared to be wanting. Unity is a note of the Church, and toleration within the net essential to its preservation. Over against Macarius he puts the violent Circumcelliones. The wicked members of the Church do not contaminate the good by a communion which is only outward and not of the heart. The threshing-floor has chaff upon it; wheat and tares must grow together. The Catholics rear the Elijah altar, the Donatist the Baal altar over against it. Christ endured Judas. Why rebaptize us, he exclaims, when you do not repeat the rite upon your once expelled but now restored Maximianists? Surely it is better to draw life from the real root. The character of him who administers the sacrament has nothing to do with its efficiency; and so he returns to the necessity for

St. Augustine

toleration within the net, as Judas was forborne in the apostolic company. The epilogue pictures the personified Church expostulating with the Donatists for quarreling with their Mother, and presents a loose summary of the previous arguments.

It is doubtful whether, even in the fashion of the times, so lengthy a poem could become a street theme, or find many repeaters in the markets and inns of Hippo or Carthage, although the refrain for peace and truthful judgment might catch the ear of the more zealous. [Cp. Retractt. I. xx.].

The Bishop of Carthage, Donatus the Great, the sphinx of Donatism, had written a book to vindicate the claim of his church to the only Christian baptism. The work obtained considerable currency, and maintained its authority, even in Augustin's day, so he answered it during the year 393, most probably, in a treatise of one book now no longer extant, but which has been given the title: "Contra Epistolam Donati hæretici," The Retractations (I. xxi.) correct some points which had been held in this work. (1). According to the Ambrosian view, Augustin here identified Peter with the rock, on which the Church was to be built; but afterwards he regarded that rock as Christ, who was the subject of the Petrine confession; on Christ was the Church to be built, and to the Church as thus reared, were given the keys. (2). The Donatus present at the Roman Synod, he had spoken of as the bishop of Carthage, the author of the book, which error is corrected in the Retractations. (3). He had also charged the writer with falsifying a favorite passage of their side, Ecclus. xxxiv. 30, but afterwards found that some codices read according to the Donatist quotation, and apologizes for his assertions.

Doubtless many of the sermons preached during his presbyterate had reference to the schism, but the chronology of these is too uncertain to allow of any definite arrangement.

We pass to the period of his co-bishopric with the aged Valerius, which dates from 395 A.D.

Evodius, a brother connected with the Church at Hippo Regius, had a chance meeting with Proculeianus, bishop of the Donatist body in that diocese. The two fell into a discussion of their mutual differences. Evodius spoke in rather a lofty and censorious way, after the fashion of his side, and wounded the feelings of the older disputant, for the Donatists, like all kindred bodies, cultivated an undue sensitiveness and were altogether too ready to take offense. Proculeianus, however, expressed a perfect readiness to have a friendly debate with Augustin in the presence of competent men. In view of this suggestion, and in the absence of Valerius, Augustin, always anxious to improve such an opening, addressed a letter to Proculeianus (c. 396), with courteous recognition, and no such sharp denial of the episcopal function as in the case of Maximin. He apologizes for the severe language of his friend, and in every way avoids any expression which might cause the tendrils again to be drawn in. The methods suggested for discussion show the anxiety of Augustin to beat out the fire of Donatism; there is the debate before chosen hearers, all the statements to be written out for use; or there is the private discussion through mutual discourse, to be read to one another and corrected, and so given to the people; or the single correspondence with a view to public lections, or any possible way that the aged bishop himself might prefer. He urges that the dead bury their dead, and the past history be left out of the debate; the present with its burning dissensions affords sufficient topics. As the people seek the bishop to arbitrate in their private litigations, let these worthies cultivate peace in this broader field; to this end he invites to prayer and conference. (Ep.xxxiii.).

Apparently, the letter led to nothing practical. A new turn was given to matters. A son had beaten his mother, and threatened her life; to avoid Catholic discipline, he joined the Donatists and was rebaptized by them: as Augustin says, he wounded also his spiritual mother by contemning her sacrament. Public registration of the facts were made by Augustin, all the more because the reported instructions, given by bishop Proculeianus to his presbyter Victor concerning the affair, had already been denied. The case presented an opportunity for getting at some rule for the recognition of one another's discipline. Accordingly Augustin addresses himself to Eusebius, a judicious Donatist of higher rank. He professes that his aim is peace; he emphasizes with impatient vehemence his opposition to coercive measures in matters of conscience: neque me id agere ut ad communionem catholicam quisquam cogatur invitus. He asks Eusebius to find out whether Proculeianus had given the order to his presbyter as recorded; whether the bishop would consent to a collation between themselves and ten selected men on each side, agreeably to the original suggestion so that the whole question might be discussed from the Scriptural grounds, not the historical. Some proposals for a meeting either at the Donatist region of Constantina, or at their projected council at Milevis, he could not accept, because both lay outside of his diocese. If Proculeianus objected to the dialectic and rhetorical skill of his counter bishop, the latter would propose Samsucius, bishop of Turris, an earnest but uncultivated man, as a substitute to lead the Catholic side. (Ep. xxxiv.).

Eusebius declined to interfere because he could not be a judge, so Augustin replies (Ep. xxxv.) that he had only asked him to make some inquiries, because the bishop refused to have any direct communication. The need for some adjustment concerning discipline had become very pressing; a Catholic sub deacon and some nuns under rebuke had been received into full standing by the Donatists, yet their subsequent career had been even more scandalous. Augustin claimed that the Catholics always respected the penal enactments of their opponents. To show his own hostility to compulsory conversions, he cites the case of a daughter, who against the paternal will had joined the Donatists, and had professed among them; when the father was about to use violence for her recall, he was dissuaded by Augustin, and when a presbyter of Proculeianus had shouted abusive epithets at him, although upon the property of a Catholic woman, he neither replied nor allowed others to resent the insult.

A practical treatise is ascribed by some to this time, called de Agone Christiano. In expounding the faith he warns against different groups of heretics and schismatics. In Chap. xxix. 31, he cautions against listening to the Donatist party, who deny the one holy Catholic church to be diffused throughout the whole world, and claim it to be alone in Africa, and there among themselves, against the plain Scripture teaching of its universality; they affirm that the prophecies of its extension have already been fulfilled, after which the whole church perished outside of their remnant. He alludes to the divisions which have befallen them as a retribution for their separation. If the end shall come after the preaching of the gospel to all nations, how can all nations have lapsed from the faith, when there remain some who are yet to hear and believe? This system robs Christ of His glory, and is to be avoided by all who love the Church. (Cp. Retractt. II. iii.).

In 397 A.D., at the death of Valerius, he became sole bishop. In this year, while on a visit to Tibursi, he had met with Glorius and other Donatists, with whom he held a friendly disputation on the origin and history of the schism, during which some Donatist documents were produced which he declared to be false, and from memory recapitulated the archives current on his side. Augustin pursued his journey to Gelizi, where he attended to some episcopal duties, and brought back with him a copy of the Catholic Gesta, and spent a day with these friends in reading them, but could not quite finish. He subsequently reproduces this story with the arguments in a letter. (Ep. xliii.). The chief burden is a criticism of the Acts, highly important in its place, but it must be passed by here save to remark that in speaking of Bishop Secundus, he suggests that it would have been better to appeal to the principalities of Rome or of some other apostolic church, than to have proceeded as he did; he should have preserved the unity at all hazards; had the case been inexplicable, he should have left it to God; if definable, he should have addressed the transmarine bishops, after finding that his peers at home could not adjust the difficulty; disobedience on the part of Cæcilian to such an order, would have made him the author of the schism; but now the Donatist altar is set up against the Universal

Church. It may be well to note that throughout the survey of these acts, there appears a manifest contradiction as to the beginning of the appellations. In the next place, the Donatists are held guilty of schism, rebaptism, and resistance to civil correction; of non-communion with those churches concerning whom they read in their lections; and of the demand for purism against the Lord's parable. The angels of the churches in the apocalypse are ecclesiastical powers, not heavenly messengers. The Church cannot be charged with the crimes of the evil men in it. Toleration is the only practice by which unity can be conserved; Moses bore with murmurers, David with Saul, Samuel with the sons of Eli, Christ with Judas. They themselves forbear with Circumcelliones, with Optatus bishop of Thamugada. The emphasis, however, is not so much upon those matters as upon schism. He would rather leave the archives and elucidate the doctrine, in which he claims to have the book of the world; that the Catholics are the Lord's inheritance; that they stand in fellowship with the churches of the New Testament; they are the light of the world. A divine rebuke has befallen Donatism in all the tenets of its particularity, by the schism and return of the Maximianists.

No open door was passed by. On a journey to Cirta, possibly about the beginning of 398 A.D., he visited with clerical friends the aged Donatist, bishop Fortunius, at Tibursi. A great company gathered who interrupted the debate; all attempts at taking notes were finally given up. In a letter (Ep. xliv.) to the Donatists, Eleusius, Glorius, and the two Felixes, who were of the number of those addressed in the previous epistle, he speaks of their witness to the conciliatory disposition of Fortunius, and recounts the substance of the interview, with the desire that it may be submitted to that bishop for correction. The discussion had opened with the question of the Church. Fortunius regretted that Augustin was not in it; the latter reversed the wish. What is the Church? Is it diffused throughout the whole world, or is it confined to Africa? Can the Donatists send letters of communion to any of the apostolic churches? Thence they dissected the Donatist claim to be the people of God, because their subjection to persecution; in which it appears that they recorded the schism of the whole world from themselves as the true Church as due to sympathy with the Macarian persecution; up to that time they had held fellowship with the whole world, and as proof thereof brought forward a letter of a council of Sardica addressed to them. From the condemnation of Athanasius and Julius by this document, Augustin, to whom it was new, concluded that this was an Arian council, and was only the more damaging to their theory. The note of persecution being resumed, he maintained that there was no approved suffering unless for a just cause, and hence the justice of the cause must first be established. Though Ambrose had endured violence at the hand of the soldiery, they would deny him to be a Christian, for they would rebaptize even him. Maximianists on the other hand were confessed to be just, although they had been dispossessed of their basilicas by the Primianist appeal to the state. As an offset, Fortunius urged the curious fact that before the election of Majorinus, an interventor had been chosen, whom the Cæcilianists put out of the way. On the following day Augustin had to confess that there was no example in the New Testament to justify compulsion in matters of faith. The next topic was Discipline. Augustin pleaded for toleration in order to keep unity. A point as to Johannic baptism sprang up, but was not pressed. From this time the debate became miscellaneous and repetitious; in its progress Fortunius confessed reluctantly that rebaptism was a fixed practice among them, and that even a Catholic bishop so highly esteemed among the Donatists for his non-persecuting spirit as was Genethlius, would have to submit to the rite before he could be recognized by their body. Augustin proposes a further examination of matters, with a view to peace, but the pacific Fortunius doubts whether many of the so-called Catholics really desire concord, to which Augustin replies that he can find ten men who would heartily enter such a conference.

On the next day the venerable Donatist calls upon his opponent to resume their talk, until an ordination called Augustin away; we also obtain information of the Cœlicolæ professing a new sort of baptism, with whose leader he desired to confer. The letter closes with a proposition to meet in the little village of Titia, near Tibursi, where there was no church, and the population pretty equally divided, and where no crowd could disturb the progress of the investigation; thither all documents should be brought and the whole subject canvassed for as long a time as it might take to terminate the discussion.

During the year Augustin issued a weighty work, which stands closely related to these visits to Fortunius. It was in two books named by himself: Contra partem Donati. Unhappily it is lost, but in the Retractations (II. v.), he says, that in the first book he had opposed the use of the secular power for compelling the schismatics to return to the communion of the State Church, a form of discipline which experience afterwards persuaded him was necessary and wholesome.

Possibly it was at the close of the year 398 that a

hint from the Donatist bishop Honoratus was brought by Herotes to Augustin, to the effect that they carry on a correspondence on the questions in dispute between them, and avoid the uproar of public debates. Augustin acquiesces heartily, and at once plunges (Ep. xlix.) into the doctrinal aspect of the matter. He begins with the note of Universality, the Church is diffused through the whole world, to establish which he brings forward some of his key passages, Ps. ii. 7, 8, Matt. xxiv. 14, Rom. i. 5. With all the apostolic churches Catholics communicate, Donatists do not. How then can this universality be limited? Why call the Catholic church Macarian, when the name of Macarius or Donatus is not known in any of these gospel regions? It rests with Donatists to prove how the Church is lost from the whole world and is confined to them. Catholics can rely on the Scriptures only for their theory. Correspondence seems to him also the better plan for discussion. Whether this mutual approach went further is not known.

It may have been in 399 A.D. that the Donatist presbyter Crispinus had met Augustin at Carthage; the two joined words, and both seem to have become heated; the former made promise to resume the parley at a later date, to the fulfillment of which the bishop had occasionally urged him. When Crispinus was elevated to the see of Calama, c. 400 A.D., and was not far from Augustin's diocese, the latter addressed him a letter (Ep. li.) rehearsing these facts. A new rumor credited Crispinus with being ready to enter the arena once more. All salutation is avoided in Augustin's letter, because the Donatists had accused him of servility. For the sake of accuracy and instruction he proposes simply to correspond, whether by one interchange of letters or by many. He pleads that present interests alone may be touched upon. Schism according to the Old Testament was more severely punished than idolatry or the burning of the sacred scroll. The charge of traditorship is set off by the acceptance of the Maximianists, whom the council of Bagai had condemned in such severe terms. If a mistake was made regarding them why not in Cæcilian's case? If these were really guilty, you consulted the wider duties of unity and toleration, and why not carry these principles farther and apply them to communion with the Catholics? As to the charge of persecution, Augustin will not enter into the merits of the matter theoretically, nor stop to plead the mildness of the measures used, but at once asks why the Donatists used the State to dislodge the Maximianists, and to deny the Catholics the possession of genuine baptism is made foolish by the recognition of the rite as existing among the Maximianists who had been cut off, and were restored without a renewal of the ceremony. The whole world had been condemned by the Donatists without an opportunity of being heard, and yet they accept the sacrament of the condemned Felicianus and Prætextatus. While they deny the validity of the symbol as administered by apostolic communions, and by the missionary churches which brought the light to Africa, they maintain that their little fraction alone is its possessor. Summarizing these arguments as a weight for the bishop to stagger under, he invokes the peace of Christ to conquer his heart.

In this same year one of his relatives, Severinus, who was a Donatist, sent a communication to him at Hippo by a special messenger, with a view of reopening friendly intercourse with his kinsman; and Augustin seizes it as a way to reestablish as well the higher kinship in Christ (Ep. lii.). The Church is an unconcealable city set on a hill; it is Catholic, being diffused throughout the whole world. The party of Donatus is cut off from the historic root of the Oriental churches, and therefore cannot bring forth the fruits of peace and love; indeed it suppresses Christ by its rebaptism. Had their charges been genuine the transmarine bishops would have supported them; at any rate they should not have withdrawn from the Unity, but rather have practiced toleration. He hopes that the bonds of custom may be broken by Severinus, and that both may find their truest relationship in Christ, since the state of schism is a despising of the eternal heritage and of perpetual salvation.

Further along in the year, a Donatist presbyter had sent to Generosus an ordo Christianitatis, or episcopal succession of Constantina, his native city, asserting that it had been delivered by an angel from heaven. About nothing were the church externalists of every camp so eager as the preservation of the succession in proof of antiquity. Generosus had only laughed at the man's stupidity, but nevertheless wrote to the bishop of Hippo about it. Fortunatus, Alypius and Augustin combine in a reply, undeniably written by the latter, commending him (Ep. liii.). The ordo Christianitatis of the whole world is theirs, from which the Donatists do not hesitate to separate themselves. This presbyter's fiction would have to be rejected at any rate, even had it come from an angel, since all other gospels than that which teaches the universality of the Church are anathema. That doctrine is in Matt. xxiv. 14, Gen. xii. 3, Gal. iii. 16. The true ordois the Roman, which he gives from Peter to Anastasius, the cotemporary pope; no Donatist is found in this list; yet as

Montenses and Cutzupitæ, they have intruded into Rome. Had there been an actual tradition, or any wicked man in the Church, that would not have vitiated the ordo, or the Church, for the law of Christ is plain, Matt. xxiii. 3, a passage again and again quoted by Augustin to substantiate this thought. They are separated from the peace of these very churches, concerning which they read in their codices, and sing pax tecum. There follows a very full and notable summary of the acts, as a refutation of the schism. He prefers the Scriptural proofs, which certify to the world-wide reach of Christ's inheritance, and its existence among all nations; from this they are separated by a nefarious schism, and charge upon the Catholics the crimes of the chaff on the threshing-floor, which must be mixed with the grain until the winnowing; these accusations do not affect the wheat which grows with the tares in the field until the end. Their divinely appointed retribution is in the history of the Maximianists, with whom they now commune, and affirm that they are not stained thereby; let them apply that lenity of judgment to the inheritance of Christ. The angel then was either Satan, or the man is Satanic, yet his salvation is desired; the sharp writing concerning him is without odium, and seeks only his correction.

Celer was a Donatist, a man of middle age and of considerable estate and civil position. He afterwards rose to the proconsulship. Augustin expresses (Ep. lvi.) a peculiar respect and affection for him, as a man of integrity and seriousness. He had desired direct instruction from the bishop, both in a matter of Christian culture and in the controversies between the two parties. Weighed down with the cares of visitation, Augustin had to delegate his presbyter Optatus to the reading and explanations of the bishop's works and views in Celer's leisure hours. The superior claims of the life beyond are set before him, together with the overwhelming force of the proofs against the schism, so that the dullest with patience and attention can get correction. The sundering of the bonds of custom and of a perversity that has become familiar, is a matter requiring great strength of character, for which step however, he, under God, would be readily capable.

But Celer was not persuaded to change his church connection by this first endeavor. On the contrary, Augustin thought he saw a laxity in the enforcement of the repressive measure ordered by the government, and so wrote a second time (Ep.lvii.). He affirms that there is no just cause for separation from that Catholic church which prophets and evangelist have declared should be diffused through the whole world. A long retained codex of Augustin, which had been loaned to Celer through Cæcilian, his own son, who seems to have been under the special tutelage of the bishop, was designed to convince the state official on this very point (we do not know which writing it may have been), should inclination or leisure lead him to its perusal, and whatever difficulties might occur, Augustin was ready to answer. He desires him also to stir up his subordinates to greater care in restoring the Catholic unity in the region of Hippo; indeed he cautions him to diligence on his own estates; a friend there, who fears to be strict in the carrying out of the statutes, could have his position alleviated by a word from Celer his patron. From this point we notice a decided sympathy with the effort to break up Donatism by force.

Parmenian, the successor of Donatus the Great in the see of Carthage, was one of the brightest disputants on their side. Against him Optatus of Milevis had directed his review of the schism, full indeed of grave historical blunders, but not lacking in that suavity which those who think they have the keys of heaven sometimes affect. When Tychonius had exposed some of the inconsequences and weaknesses of the Donatist theory of the Church, Parmenian undertook a reply, whose main object was to fortify the propositions, (1) that the evil defile the good in the Church, and must therefore be cut off; and (2) that puristic folly, that the Donatist community was absolutely pure in its membership and priesthood. To this much-esteemed work, Augustin replies (c. 400 A.D.) in three books: Contra Epistolam Parmeniani.

In Book I. the main question is, who really incurred the guilt of schism, and initiated the appeal to the State? He opens with the praise of Tychonius as man and author, but misses the acute drift of that great man's argument. He seeks to answer the data of the origin of the separation as given by Parmenian, who attributes it to the joint movement of Gaul, Spain and Italy in seeking to make their views universal, and to the influence of Hosius over Constantine, in winning him to their opinion; nor does Parmenius cease to deprecate the imperial intervention. Augustin defends this use of the secular arm, but accuses the Donatists by their history of beginning it in the appeal to Constantine, in the treatment of the Rogatists and Maximianists, in the abuses of the Circumcelliones, in their petition to Julian.

Book II. discusses the texts alleged by the Donatists in support of the purity of the Church, the need of discipline, the sole validity of their baptism and ordination, the blamelessness of their members and clergy. While both fail in exegetical principles, Parmenian, after the manner of his school, is aggravatingly guilty of using mere catch-words, without regard to text or context. He quotes indiscriminately whatever sounds favorable to his cause. Some of the passages are: Is. v. 20, Prov. xvii. 15, Is. lix. 1–8, Ecclus. x. 2, Is. lxvi. 3, Prov. xxi. 27, and others. Augustin gives his interpretations, and does not fail to prod his opponent with barbs of Optatus, Maximianists, and Circumcelliones.

Book III. handles further the theory of purism in the light of Scriptural proofs. The first part is mainly an endeavor to give the true significance of I Cor. v. 12, 13. (Compare his correction in the Retractt. II. xvii.). Augustin is constrained to confess the need of some internal discipline, and then enforces with wider range the notes of universality, unity and toleration, especially as illustrated by Cyprian. [Cp. Retractt.. II. xvii.].

In the work against Parmenian, he had promised to write more fully on this subject of baptism, the frequent persuasions of the brethren also moved him so that in this same year (400 A.D.) he issued the seven books De Baptismo: Contra Donatistas. The double purpose is to define that sacrament as the property of Christ, and to overthrow the Donatist appeal to the authority of Cyprian and the famous council of Carthage, with its eighty-seven deliverances in favor of the repetition of the rite. Since this is one of the works translated in the accompanying volume any further analysis may be passed by. [Cp. Retractt. II. xviii.].

In this period of frequent and heated controversy, a Donatist layman, Centurius by name, brought some of their quotations and writings, and supported with

Scriptural proofs to the Church in Hippo. It seems to have begun with an exposition of Prov. ix. 17. (N. Afr. version and LXX). Augustin answered them briefly in a tractate, which he entitles: Contra quod attulit Centurius a Donatistis. It is however not extant. In the Retractations (II. xix.) it is placed immediately after the work on Baptism.

Meanwhile, and as the Retractations tell us, before he had finished his work on the Trinity, and his literal commentary on Genesis, he found it desirable to reply to the pastoral letter of Petilian, Donatist bishop of Constantina; unfortunately only a part of the epistle came into his hand, so strenuous and vigilant were the efforts to hide their literature from the eyes of this ardent foe. He replied with one book to so much as he had received, c. 400 A.D. Some of his clergy subsequently obtained and wrote out a complete copy, so that he composed the second book, c. 401 A.D. Meanwhile Petilian responded to the first issue, and this necessitated a third book, c. 401 or 402 A.D. The three books were collected into one treatise, and are known under the title Contra Litteras Petiliani. The main object of the series is the refutation of Petilian's proposition: "Conscientia namque (sancte) dantis attenditur, quæ (qui) abluat accipientis." "Nam qui fidem (sciens) a perfido sumpserit, non fidem percipit, sed reatum." "What we look for is the conscience of the giver (him who gives in holiness), to cleanse that of the recipient." "For he who (wittingly) receives faith from the faithless receives not faith, but guilt." Since the work is also a part of this volume, we need not dwell on it farther. [Cp. Retractt. II. xxv.]

The civil restraints were applied with vigor on the one side and resented on the other by the retaliatory

Circumcelliones. To Pammachius, a man of senatorial rank, Augustin, in 401 A.D., sends a letter [Ep. lviii.] of exuberant congratulations and flatteries, because he had compelled some of his Numidian tenants to return to the mother Church; a converting agency which he condemns unmercifully when practiced by the Donatists. The plan, he says, would have been urged upon other landholders, had the clergy not been afraid of the scornful finger of the Donatists, who were in such favor with the proprietors, that an effort like this might have failed. He desires the senator to circulate this letter wherever there was promise of effect. The bishop, now thoroughly committed to these arbitrary procedures, was in some trepidation lest the plausible arguments which the Donatists were urging, might shake the resolution of Pammachius himself, and so he sends a secret commission of instruction.

The coercive measures yielded fruit, and the question about the status of recedent Donatist clergy now became pressing. Augustin had already met with a certain Theodore on this subject, and in a letter addressed to him [Ep. lxi.] c. 401, recapitulated the proposition then agreed upon, to be used as a basis for treatment with all who wanted to come over. The Catholic church opposed only the schism and the rebaptism among the Donatists; what was good she was ready to acknowledge. Baptism itself, ordination, self-denial, celibacy, doctrinal views, especially as to the Trinity, these were confessedly right, only to reap the profit of them, it was essential for Donatists to be in the unity and in the root.

The Council of Carthage of September 13, 401, adopted this view, Can. 2. There had also been a remarkable scarcity of Catholic clergy, so that application had been made to Rome and Milan for relief; probably this had its influence upon so charitable a view of schismatic ordination.

It was alleged that Crispinus, the bishop of Calama, had bought a state farm at Mappalia, and had rebaptized the tenants. Augustin was roused by this counter-irritant and wrote him a letter, c. 402 A.D. [Ep. lxvi.], wondering what he would do if the authorities were to impose the fine for every offense. He pleads for an answer to Christ, whose was all the world, because bought with his blood, while the Donatist would affirm that Christ had lost all the world save Africa. He urges a public discussion of the mooted points before these converts, which should be reported and done into Punic as a test of their freedom in this conversion, and frankly enough offers to do the same for any case of coercion on his side. Unless Crispinus and his helpers acquiesce, he will hold them guilty.

The uppermost talk of those times was the extraordinary charity of the Donatists toward the Maximianists. One form of apology for such a seeming vacation of all their tenets was to say, e.g., of Felicianus of Musti, that he was ignorantly condemned when innocent and absent, so in his absence, he was reinstated. This statement was made by a Donatis bishop, Clarentius, in reply to the inquiries of Naucelio. Alypius and Augustin, who were made aware of this defense, urged in criticism [Ep. lxx.] that the Council of Bagai was therefore guilty in condemning Felicianus unheard, and all the more in that they afterward found him to be innocent. Either he ought not to have been condemned if he was innocent, or if guilty, he ought not to have been received back. If the council erred, why not apply such a liability to error to the origin of the schism; might not

Cæcilian, unheard, have been condemned although innocent? But, as a matter of fact, Felicianus was found guilty while in thorough and declared sympathy with Maximian, and the state was called upon to enforce his ejection. If he was welcomed without rebaptism, why not treat the Church diffused through the whole world with the same consideration?

It was probably in the year 402 that he addressed a general appeal to the Donatist [Ep. lxxvi.], not to endanger their salvation by continuance in schism. If they counted the surrender of the sacred books so great a sin, how much more grievous a transgression ought the refusal to obey the plain commands of these books as to unity be considered. He brings forward the usual array of passages to demonstrate the universality of the Church, and that any limitation of this note, can only be at the end of the world. The attempt to separate the wheat from the tares before the harvest, is only a proof that they are of the tares. A rapid survey of the origin of the schism follows, and all the archives are made to tell against them. He asks how they can hold any theory of purism while they regard Optatus as a martyr and welcome the excommunicated Maximianists? Schism in the Scriptures is punished more severely than the burning of the books. Why complain about traditorship when Maximianists are received? Why abuse the imperial laws directed against them, when they had invoked the same against the Maximianists? If theirs is the only baptism, what is the baptism of these Maximianists, which is without question validated? He challenges the Donatist bishops to discuss these matters with their laity, if they persist in declining to meet the Catholics, and bids the sheep beware of the wolves and their den.

Writings in Connection with the Donatist Controversy - Introductory Essay

The ad Catholicos Epistola, popularly known as de Unitate Ecclesiæ, is generally attributed to Augustin, and is addressed to the brethren of his charge; it may be taken as a contrast to the previous letter directed to the Donatists, and not unlikely saw the light in 402 A.D. This book is designed as a continuance of the controversy with Petilian, and indeed a further correspondence is proposed, so that the work must have appeared before that bishop's death, which is generally placed in this year. The chief question between the two parties is, Where is the Church? Is it with Catholic or Donatist? The Church is one and Catholic: it is the body of Christ, consisting of Him as its Head and those in Him as members. The historical issue in any of four possibilities of truth or falsity does not justify separation from this body. The point is, What does the Lord say? The Donatist should believe in the books, which he says were delivered up, and put aside all other documents except the divine canons. Do the Scriptures say that the Church is in Africa only, and in the few Cutzupitanæ or Montenses at Rome, and in the house or patrimony of one woman in Spain, or is it in the whole world? A second time does he start out with a definition of the Church, as having for its head the Only Begotten Son, and for its body the members in Him; as bridegroom and bride, two in one flesh. Any divergence from the Head or the body, whether caused by difference in doctrine or government, is per se outside of the Church. He meets the two favorite Donatistic comparisons of the divine institution with the ark and Gideon's fleece, and then enlarges upon the note of universality, with included unity, by Scripture texts from the Law, the Prophets, especially Isaiah, and the Psalms. From the Donatist position these are not fulfilled, because, say they, men are unwilling. Men were created with free will; they believe or disbelieve according to that. When the Church began to increase in the world, men refused to persevere, and the Christian religion was lost from all the nations except for the Donatists. All this, replies Augustin, as if the Spirit of God did not know the future volitions of men. But Christ, after the resurrection, said that the Law, the Prophets and the Psalms testified of Him, and that the fulfillment of his kingdom should begin from Jerusalem. He then follows out the expansion of the Church as given in the Acts, and the foundation of Christian communities as mentioned in the Epistles and the Revelation. The Donatists reply to this theory of development that the Church perished save among them in North Africa. It is among the few: for which they cite a similar state of things under Enoch, Noah, Lot, Abraham, Isaac, and Jacob, and the Kingdom of Judah. The spread of the Church did indeed begin from Jerusalem, but afterwards an apostasy befell it, in the progress of which the communion of the Donatists alone remained faithful. Augustin says the fact that there are evil persons in the Church is simply a proof of the fulfillment of those parables of our Lord, which illustrate the mixed characters in his kingdom. There is indeed a paucity of the good, but within that communion. Then follows a discussion of the geographical limitation, the Donatists maintaining that the Oriental churches and the rest mentioned in the sacred canon had receded from the faith. Especially is their favorite paragraph, a passage from Cant. i. 7, commented upon. He presses the continuous preaching among all nations, after which event the end is to come; there must be such a universal growth to that end. Let us cease drawing from the acts and sayings of men about this great matter, and take the simple testimony of the Scriptures. But the Donatists object: If the Church be among you why do you compel us by force to enter its peace? Or if we are evil why do you desire us? and if we are tares why hinder us from growing until the harvest? Augustin then justifies the system of correction adopted in loving care for their salvation, not failing to remind them of the Circumcelliones and their own action about the Maximianists. Another inquiry of the Donatists was, How will you recognize us if we come to you? Augustin says, as the universally founded Church is wont to receive, put away all hatred and your sacraments are acknowledged. This leads to the discussion of baptism and of that related topic, the effect, of the celebrant's character, upon the recipient. He returns finally to the note of universality as essential to the unity, with the one Head and the one body.

Somewhere about 404 A.D. two official cases of discipline had occurred in Augustin's monasterium, which had grieved the pride of the clergy, because they had boasted of their establishment as purer than the puristic body gathered about the Donatist bishop Proculeianus. They were more troubled about this than about the sins of the suspected brethren, one of whom, however, seemed to have considerable injustice done him. While discussing this matter [in Ep. lxxviii.] he incidentally mentions the lapse of two Donatists, who had been received into Augustin's communion, and whose conduct the clergy had regarded as a proof of the laxity of discipline under Proculeianus.

A sermon on the 95th Ps. (96) may have been preached in the year 404 or thereabouts, in which he rebukes the Donatists for their pride in claiming either that they, the few in Africa, are the ones bought by Christ, or that they are so great because this large gift was bestowed on them alone. And in commenting on v. 10, dicite in nationibus, Dominus regnavit a ligno, etc., he twits them with seeking this reign by the wood through the cudgels of the Circumcelliones; and enlarges too upon the theme of universality, against their undiscoverable here and there.

Cæcilianus, whose exact civil office, whether vicar or præfectus annonæis yet undetermined, Augustin addresses as præsesin Ep. lxxxvi., which is ascribed to 405 A.D. The severer edicts of Honorius had just been published. This official had carried them out with telling earnestness. His administration in the greater part of Africa is particularly commended; the bishop begs of him to restore the Catholic unity also in Hippo and the frontiers of Numidia. The ill-success of his own work is not due to lack of episcopal duty, and he asks Cæcilianus to inquire of the clergy, or of the bearer, a commissioned presbyter, about the true state of matters; he would have the State begin with monitions in the hope of preventing a resort to severer remedies.

Emeritus, the bishop of Julia Cæsarea, one of the seven Donatist disputants at the later conference, did not shun correspondence or association with his opponents. He is described as a man of parts and character. Augustin had written a letter to him, which is not preserved, and it had received no reply. He once more seeks to win him to a friendly discussion or correspondence [Ep. lxxxvii.], in this time of general return to the mother Church. He would have all men of culture come back to the true fellowship. What Emeritus's particular ground for continuing in separation maybe he does not know. He proceeds to discuss universality, purism, the validity of the documents, the heinousness of schism, the paucity of numbers, and the right of coercion.

The enforcement of the civil edicts was followed by violent outbreaks of the Circumcelliones, especially in Augustin's diocese. The clergy united in a protest [Ep. lxxxviii.] addressed to the venerable Bishop Januarius, a Donatist, probably in 406 A.D. They claim (1) that they are receiving evil for good. (2) The appeal to the state was begun by the Majorinists, and two full documents are given in proof. (3) All decrees of the empire since, are the simple execution of the edict of Constantine against the party of Donatus which these had wanted to be issued against Cæcilian. (4) The acts of the Circumcelliones; were the real occasion for sharper efforts at suppression; instances of their cruelty are mentioned. (5) The Catholics have pursued a conciliatory policy by conferences and by desiring a mitigation of the penalties, which were frustrated the one by refusals, the other by a gross assault on the Catholic bishop of Bagai; all who come into the hands of the state clergy, are treated with merciful persuasion. (6) Various proposals for peace are suggested.

Festus, a government official and a landed proprietor apparently in Hippo, had written a letter urging a return of the Donatists to the mother Church. It bore little fruit, and he asks Augustin first to instruct him and also to give him a tractate for general use. Augustin, c. 406. [Ep. lxxxix.], enforces the duty of perseverance in the civil reclamation of the Donatists; their claim of persecution as a note attesting them to be the true people of God is folly, because it is not the mere suffering but the cause for which one suffers that makes a martyr. He exhorts him to read the archives and see how the schismatics initiated the appeal to the secular power, and how all things that have befallen them through that arm would have been the just fate of the Cæcilianists, had the Donatist course been approved. Besides, why this unjust treatment of the Church universal in condemning it unheard, and rebaptizing its members, who have done them no wrong? The theory that baptism alone is valid when administered by the just, is putting a trust in man which the Scriptures condemn; the sacrament is not man's but Christ's; further, one would prefer to be baptized by a bad man, for then he would receive grace from Christ directly, according to their subterfuge. He is vexed with their active and passive opposition; the mother has to correct, although her obstinate child may not like it. They aver that the Catholics accept them without requiring any change in them, but the change required is great, no less a one than from error to truth. The bishop proposes as a substitute for Festus's plan, the sending of an authorized messenger secretly to himself, and they would devise together a method for the correction of the Donatists.

In the second sermon on Ps. cii. (ci.) preached about this time, when enlarging upon the unity he ridicules the Donatist assertion that the Church which was among all the nations had perished, as the impudent voice of those who are not in it declares. So is their affirmation that Scripture prophecies about the spread of the kingdom have been fulfilled; all nations have believed, but this diffused communion apostatized and perished. He rebukes the conceit that the Lord's saying, I am with you, even to the end of the world, was designed for them alone, the Lord foreseeing that the party of Donatus would be in the earth. If emperors have propounded laws against heretics, it is a part of the predictions which foretold how kings would serve the Lord. Thence he expands the notes of universality and perpetuity.

Cresconius, a layman and philologist, read Augustin's first book in answer to Petilian, and wrote a reply, which, however, was circulated among the Donatists only. Augustin at last secured a copy, and wrote (406 A.D., some say as late as 409) Contra Cresconium Grammaticum Partis Donati, libri IV. Three of these books controvert the arguments of Cresconius; part of the third and the fourth entire is a detailed polemic history of the Maximian schism.

In Book I. he alludes to the occasion of the writing, and hesitates between being regarded as contumelious if he declined an answer, and arrogant, should he reply. Cresconius had attacked eloquence, which Augustin defends as simply the art of speaking, and as not to be condemned because it has been abused. You do not condemn military armament for your country because others have taken up arms against the country; the physician does not refuse to use all drugs because some are baneful; because there are sophists one is not to deny the value of eloquence. Cresconius seemed to regard its cultivation as injurious to the simplicity of Christian law and teaching. He also had accused Augustin of persistent arrogance in his pertinacious pursuit of the Donatists. Augustin claims to do a good work with good ends in view, and says its fruit has been a rich harvest for the Church. So the discussion passes on to the use of dialectics, which Cresconius assails, but Augustin defends as nothing else than a demonstration of results, either the true from the true or the false from the false. He justifies not disputatiousness, but the arguments by which truth is built up, for Christ employed it, and St. Paul wielded its weapons not only with the Jews but with Epicureans and Stoics. In all this we have an illustration of that unfortunate tendency to undervalue culture whenever a puristic community passes into the fires. Augustin applies the art to one of the points which Cresconius had discussed, viz., rebaptism. He had endeavored to prove that it was solely among them. Augustin concedes that the rite is there, but not its profit; in order to enjoy its profit, it must be administered lawfully. The oneness of baptism as a ceremony is not dependent on the oneness of the Church, whereas its profit is. A reprobate society of heretics can have a good baptism, but it is not properly and not profitably administered among them; the proper and profitable administration is solely in the Church to salvation; the rite outside is to judgment.

In Book II. after a résumé of the previous book, he notices first the criticism as to the true construction of the name Donatistœ; it should rather be Donatiani as Cresconius claimed. He is ready to concede this, and in his controversy with the philologist will use that form, but on all other occasion he would prefer the more familiar termination. Cresconius also protests against the term heretic as applied to them, which he regards as a divergence of views from the Christian faith; while a schism has sprung up among those for whom the same Christ was born, died and rose again, who have one religion, the same sacraments, and no diversity in Christian observance. Augustin, however, while not particularly dwelling on these agreements, presses upon him the articles of divergence, and asks why they rebaptize? The recognition of Donatist ordination concerning which Cresconius had asked, Augustin declares to be a matter of charity. As to the question of Cresconius, Why, if the Donatists are such heretics and so sacrilegious, if they are indeed guilty of a nefarious and inexpiable crime, some purification is not adopted when they come over to the Catholic church? Augustin answers: We do not regard it as inexpiable, and baptism is not to be repeated, it is Christ's; on coming to us the Donatist receives the Spirit signified by that rite; he begins to have healthfully what he previously had hurtfully and unworthily. The relation of the celebrant to the symbol as presented by Cresconius is a modification of Petilianism. "Regard is had," says he, "to the conscience of the giver, not according to its actuality, which cannot be perceived but according to his reputation, whether that be true or false." Augustin does not fail to crowd him for the change of base. The favorite passages of Ps. cxli. 5, Jer. xv. 18, and Ecclus. xxxiv. 31, are gone over. Then he answers the charge made by Cresconius, as to the right of any sinner to baptize among the Catholics. Finally, he reviews Cyprian's relation to rebaptism, who is not a canonical authority for him; the Scriptures alone are such; but the Donatists ought to consider that decision of his to remain in unity from the fact that the mixed nature of its membership requires toleration.

  Book III. Augustin contends that the Donatists by their schism from especially the Eastern churches had violated the principle of toleration, which their boasted leader had so strenuously enforced. There follows then a seriatim consideration of the points made by Cresconius, like those maintained by Petilian, as to the importance of the origin and the head and root in baptism, or the character of the celebrant, and the rebaptism by Paul of John's disciples. The case of Optatus and the Maximianists next come under review, as witnesses against their testimonies. Cresconius says he will neither absolve nor condemn Optatus, and as to the Maximianists, he professes to have made special inquiry into the whole history. The Synod had granted a season of delay during which all who returned should be held innocent. Of this very many availed themselves; the baptism of these was valid; those who remained outside lost both baptism and the church. Augustin refutes the statement from its inherent contradictions and from the language of the Synod against the Maximianists. Cresconius also brings forward the Sardican council's letter to Donatus as a proof of sustained fellowship. Augustin declares it to be an Arian council; and he insists on paralleling all Cresconius would say about Cæcilianism with the career of the Maximianists. With reference to persecution, he cites in extensor their own persecutions, the case of Severus, bishop of Thubursicubur; the acts of Optatus; his own treatment at a collation by the Circumcelliones; the case of Crispinus, the Donatist bishop of Calama; their own invocation of the state against the Maximianists. Thence he returns to the doctrine of the unity as universal with many of the familiar Scripture texts, and asserts by the documents that the Donatists were the occasion of the rupture.

  Book IV. is a review of Cresconius's work by the light of the Maximianist records. Beginning with a pleasantry as to their eloquence and dialectic spirit, he follows in detail the points of Cresconius whether doctrinal or historical as to Cæcilian, mainly with

Maximianist data as offsets. Cresconius charges Augustin with having called Petilian Satan, and so violating the peace he professes. Augustin claims that he only compared the error not the person, to Satan. Nor had Cresconius forgotten to bring out the Manichæism of his opponent. Augustin reminds him both of what he had written against them and also of what sins were forgiven in the return of Maximian, who was an old man when Augustin was but young; these were the sins of his youth. The theories of fellowship, of persecution, of baptism, are all considered in the light of their own council of Bagai and its sequences. [Cp. Retractt.II. xxvi.].

After concluding his work against Cresconius, he issued, probably in this same year, a little treatise he had promised, containing a collection of proofs both for Donatist and Catholic popular use. To the pledge itself an unknown Donatist replied, which led to the production of a second book, whose title Augustin designed to be: Contra nescio quem Donatistam. The original promise was fulfilled in the publication of the Probationes et Testimonia contra Donatistas, embracing all the ecclesiastical and public acts and Scripture proofs bearing on the questions between them. It was designed mainly for public reading in the basilicas. Both were joined in one book, although apparently afterwards separated. In each he confesses to the error of placing the purgation of Felix after instead of before the vindication of Cæcilian. At this writing he still regarded the Donatists as psychics and babes, but in his old age corrects his application of the words to them, since he came to consider them rather as dead and lost. Unfortunately neither treatise has been preserved. [Cp. Retractt. II. xxvii. and xxviii.].

He also conceived the plan of preparing a polemic

for the people who had little time for extended reading, by refuting the entire theory of the schism through the story of the excision and restoration of the Maximianists. It appeared c. 406 A.D. under the name of Admonitio Donatistarum de Maximianistis: this too is lost. [Cp. Retractt. II. xxix.]. An acquaintance of earlier days in Carthage, Vincentius, had become bishop of the little Rogatist fragment as the immediate successor of Rogatus himself at Cartenna. He, or someone of that little band, had written a letter to Augustin with a pretty strong plea against persecution. This was not unlikely in c. 408 A.D., and Augustin answers in one of his most weighty epistles (Ep.xciii.), under the supposition that Vincentius was the author, and vindicates the help of the State. Evidently a change had come over Numidia, for he boasts of the multitudes who had been converted, and rejoices in the fruitful use of the secular arm for their salvation. Even Circumcelliones had become steadfast Catholics. Coercion stimulates the thoughtless and those bound by custom, and delivers these held back by fear; it is like a wholesome medicine, or the wounds inflicted by a friend. God chastens in order to better the life and to bring men to repentance. The householder instructs us to compel them to come in. Sarah and Hagar are types; so the mother Church corrects her children. Everything depends on the aim in persecution, whether it be done for oppression or for good; it is the difference between Pharaoh and Moses in their treatment of Israel. The Father gave up the Son, and the Son gave Himself up; while Judas betrayed Him. The righteousness of the end for which one suffers alone constitutes martyrdom. The Rogatist is not suffering for righteousness but for unrighteousness. Augustin is constrained to confess that there are no persecutions recorded in the New Testament as inflicted by Christians, but explains the omission as due to the fact that rulers were not yet members of the Church. He thinks, too, that the moderate and discriminating form of the correction employed, helps to justify a resort thereto. If the Rogatists have nothing to do with the violence of the Circumcelliones, and use no force as the rest of the Donatists do, it is because they are so few and feeble. The Donatists, however, did use the secular arm against the Maximianists, and in the appeal to Julian. He will not allow a distinction between resort to law for the recovery of property and for the coercion of the conscience. He claims that to regain one's own in this way has no apostolic warrant. The Donatists, too, sought imperial aid to coerce Cæcilianus. Why shall not Catholics return in kind? The very edict of confiscation which had hit them they had hoped might fall on the head of Cæcilian and his followers. What Tychonius said describes the very essence of Donatist arbitrariness: quod volumus sanctum est. The sin of separation from the whole world followed; the universal church was condemned unheard, and the toleration which Cyprian urged disregarded. He traces his own change of views from the non-coercive to the coercive policy, the success of the method in hastening conversions won him wholly as an enthusiastic and persistent supporter. He bids Vincentius flee from the wrath to come. What is his little handful compared with the universal Church? This note of universality he develops in extensor against their limitation, and especially their new definition of Catholic, as obedience to all the laws and the sacraments, and to their childish allegory of Cant. i. 7. He hints that in the ancient times there might have been a little schism which anticipated the Rogatists, and which had called itself exclusively the Church. He thinks it is also the duty of the State to suppress idolatry. The passage quoted from Hilary by Vincentius, as to the few who in Asia in his day were believers despite the spread of the Church, Augustin softens into an excited picture of the dark times of persecution. Next, he discusses the position of Cyprian. All patristic testimony, however, is of no final value; the only authority is the Word of God. Moreover, if Cyprian be quoted, why not on the side of his love for unity and toleration? The averment that the Church, except for the Rogatists, perished by fellowship with the unbaptized, is met with the fact that in Cyprian's time men had been received without rebaptism into the Church, and therefore the Church, according to their theory, must have perished before their day; if it, however, survived that condition, then there is no excuse left for a schism on that ground. One is not of higher merit than Cyprian simply because he may abhor that father's error, any more than they who did not fall into Peter's mistake are above him in worth on that account. Indeed, Cyprian may have rectified his fault before death; and some say that those passages are interpolations. Augustin, however, concedes their authenticity. Cyprian, in his Epistle to Antonianus, shows how the African bishops maintained unity despite the corrupt lives of some colleagues; variations of opinion were allowed; neither were they contaminated by such a fellowship, nor was the Church destroyed. Tychonius states the result of a Donatist council which granted fellowship to those in their own body who had been guilty of tradition, and that without rebaptism, in case the restored should oppose such a repetition of the rite.

Deuterius, bishop of Macriana, had admitted traditors to his communion without renewing the sacrament, and many witnesses of both facts were living in Tychonius's own day. Parmenian had indeed replied to the arguments, but could not gainsay the facts. Augustin professes in all sincerity his anxiety for the salvation of the jeopardized Donatists; the Church acknowledges the Sacrament which they have administered, and desires them to have the profit thereof. In defense of rebaptism Vincentius had alleged the case of Paul, repeating the ceremony after John. Augustin asks was John then a heretic? If not, it is for you to say why the ordinance was iterated; Christ's baptism is always the same and must not be iterated; it has nothing to do with the merit or demerit of the individual, or else Paul would not have declined its continuous administration. He begs him to put no confidence in the accident of their being a little company, and not to arrogate to themselves the title of Catholic, in the sense of being keepers of the entire law and all the sacraments, nor to peculiar sanctity as the few who were to have faith at the coming of the Son of Man. The Church does not take pleasure in correction, save for conversion; she abhors those who seek Donatist property out of sheer covetousness, yet all property does belong to the true Church. She has also no delight in any who disregard Donatist discipline, by receiving members who have been ejected from that body for sin. The Catholic Church sustains the unity, and recognizes the mixture of chaff and wheat, good and bad fish, the goats and the sheep. He bids him come to that Church into whose fellowship Vincentius had described Augustin as entering. He closes with reflections on the aggravations in the sin of schism and on the need of repentance.

Olympius had recently been elevated to the dignity of magister officiorum. He had written to Augustin soliciting his advice on the best way for the civil authority to help the Church. Augustin, c. 408 [Ep. xcvii.], welcomes his elevation, commends his devotion to the body of Christ, and is glad to have his own timidity relieved by this invitation to lay before the highest official the exacting needs of the hour. These had become grave; the very success of coercion had precipitated new commotions among the Circumcelliones and their clerical abettors. A commission had sailed in mid-winter to solicit imperial help against their fury. The first point he would suggest, but without having had the opportunity of consultation, save probably with bishop Severus, is to declare by proclamation that the imperial edicts were not the invention of Stilicho, as the Donatists and heathen boasted. As to further plans, the episcopal commission would doubtless consult with him on their return from court. He invites Olympius to rejoice with him on the practical benefits of coercion thus far.

It may have been a little later (c. 408 or 409) that Augustin writes to Donatus the proconsul (Ep. c.) regretting indeed that the Church must avail herself of the State, but he is gratified that so devoted a son is wielding the sword for her. The crimes against the Church are greater than all other crimes, but in her discipline he deprecates any spirit of revenge, and pleads most beseechingly against the infliction of capital punishment; that would be a deterrent to the bringing in of any charges against the guilty. He asks for a republication of the repressive laws, since the enemy is boasting of their repeal.

Augustin wrote a general letter to the Donatist

people in c. 409 [Ep.cv.], in which he declares that the Catholic effort at their conversion is the work of peacemakers. Some Donatist presbyters had ordered the Catholics to let their people alone, if they did not want to be killed, but Augustin would all the rather ask the people to recede from the schismatics because they were separated from that body for which Christ died. Catholics must seek for the stolen sheep that had on them the mark of Christ. The charge of being traditors, says he, we meet with a like accusation against you, and then you bid us leave. You claim to be the Church on this unproved charge, unmindful of what law, prophecy, Psalms, Apostles and Gospels say as to its universality beginning at Jerusalem. You are not in communion with that universal body, and you prevent the escape of others from a similar perdition. The objection as to persecution he meets with an invitation to look at the deeds of clergy and Circumcelliones, and cites instances of grievous ill-treatment toward voluntary converts: Marcus, presbyter of Casphalia, Restitutus of Victoria, Marcianus of Urga, Maximinus and Possidius, and then protests against their general violence and robberies, and especially against attributing martyrdom to those who had only been punished for their crimes. To all this compulsion we oppose the State, he affirms, and many of your own people rejoice in deliverance from your oppressions. You have filled Africa with false charges as to Cæcilian, Felix, etc., and though we do not place our hope in man, yet we do recognize the State as the servant of the Church. Nebuchadnezzar is an example both of the persecutor and the correctionist. You despise the baptism of Christ; ought this not to be punished? He then reviews the history of the case in the light of the documents;

commenting on them as forms of their own appeal to the State. The liberty of error is most deadly to the soul. Christ and the Apostles command unity, and this command the Emperors seek to enforce. Only Julian and the heathen emperors were persecutors; the only martyrs are those who suffer for Catholic truth. The whole imperial legislation against Donatism is the outcome of the original statute of Constantine and sprang after all from their appeal. He next discusses their view of baptism and insists that the rite is independent of the character of the celebrant; were it dependent, then, according to their notion, we should rather desire to be baptized by a bad man, in order to receive the grace directly from Christ. The appeal to unity follows. Make concord with us he urges; we love you and desire to serve you, even by the aid of the temporal laws; we do not want you to perish as aliens from your Catholic mother. Your charges you are unable to substantiate, and yet you avoid all conference with us, as if to shun fellowship with sinners; a false pride, which is rebuked by Paul's conduct, by the Lord's in his treatment of Judas; the Lord held conference even with the devil. This he follows with extended Scriptural proofs of the universality of the Church. He reminds them again of the unproved charges which apply rather to themselves; but he has no desire for the historical argument, rather for the doctrinal. The Catholic aim is their conversion, whether by the persuasion of argument or the correction of laws. They should remember the mixed nature of the Church, and that mere contact with evil does not defile. If you hold to Christ, hold also to His Church; you kill us who seek to tell you the truth, and do not want you to perish in evil. May God vindicate us and his cause by slaying your errors and making you rejoice with us in the truth.

On the death of Proculeianus, Macrobius succeeded to the see of Hippo Regius. Augustin hears that he is about to rebaptize a sub deacon (Rusticianus) who under discipline left the Catholics. Augustin urges him [Ep. cvi.], c. 409, not to do this by his desire to have life in God, and to please God by not making the sacraments vain, and by his hope of not being separated from the body of Christ eternally. The Donatists have admitted the validity of baptism as administered by Felicianus and Primianus, why then rebaptize others? and begs him to search that case as a test of the whole matter.

Maximus and Theodore had been commissioned to deliver the previous letter to Bishop Macrobius. He at first declined to listen to its reading, but was at last persuaded to attend, and in reply said: It was his duty to receive all who came, and to give faith to those who asked it. Into the question about Primian he would not enter, because of his own recent ordination; he was not a judge of his father, and he would remain in what his predecessors had accepted. These replies were conveyed to Augustin in the letter cvii. (c. 409) by the two commissioners.

In still further hope of reaching Bishop Macrobius, Augustin addressed another epistle, (cviii.) c. 409, to him in answer to the objections offered by him at the interview with the commissioners. 1. As to the point that he must receive those who come and give them the faith they ask: Augustin proposes the case of someone who has received the rite in their communion, but had been separated from it for a time, and having returned, conscientiously desires to be rebaptized; Macrobius, according to his objection, could not repeat the rite, but would proceed to instruct him. Why repeat it when Augustin administers it? Maybe you will quote, "keep thyself from strange water and do not drink from a strange fountain." How then will you explain the reception of Felicianus? 2. As to the second conclusion, that you would remain in the faith of your predecessors: It is a pity for a young man of good parts to say so; nothing compels you to remain in evil; you had better be in the Church which began in Jerusalem and spread thence through the world. 3. And if you will not judge your fathers why judge my fathers? If not Primian, why Cæcilian? Why deny us to be brethren? why rend the body? why extinguish the baptism of Christ, who baptizes with the Spirit, and who gave Himself for the Church? Yet your colleagues in effect do yield to the truth in their recognition of the Maximianists. Judge not the evil but do judge what was good in Primian. That act of his, the reception of the Maximianists, absolves the nations who are ignorant of what you accuse us. He then traces the whole development of that schism and its overthrow, to show that those schismatics were not rebaptized at their return. That history Augustin considers a divinely appointed refutation of all the Donatist tenets. He proceeds to criticize their Scripture proofs, Prov. ix. 18, Jer. xv. 18, Eccl. xxxiv. 30, Ps. cxli. 5, which he turns against them through the story of the schism. He next addresses himself to their theory of fellowship, and discusses their proof texts, I Tim. v. 22, Is. lii. 11, I Cor. v. 6; Ezekiel, Daniel, the Apostles, Christ and Paul all rebuke this purism. Cyprian's authority for rebaptism is reviewed. Augustin repeats the doubts of very many as to the authenticity of those parts of his works which favor this view; but granted that they are valid, Cyprian, nevertheless, maintained unity and toleration, and by martyrdom purged his mistake. There is, however, no martyrdom outside of the unity, as that father also testified. Cyprian acknowledged as well the presence of many evil persons in the ministry and in the Church, but stood to it that unity must not be sacrificed on that account. The Church is a mixed society; this is Christ's law. Had Macrobius's associates remembered the parable of the wheat and tares they would not have separated. This argument is concluded with a sort of summary of the points traversed before. As to the note of persecution: that alone is a martyrdom which surrenders the life for a good cause. The Donatists too used the State in the case of the Maximianists, and to them belong the Circumcelliones. The matter of unity and the connected points of toleration and fellowship are again enlarged upon.

A sermon attributed to Augustin, De Rusticiano subdiacono a Donatistis rebaptizato et in diaconum ordinato, falls in the same year, 409, with the letter to Bishop Macrobius. There is an outburst of deep grief over the act. It would appear that Rusticianus had been a special favorite of Augustin, on whom he had expended much care; but he had become involved in scurrilous deeds, in feasting and intemperance, day and night, and was plunged in debt, and at last was excommunicated by his presbyter, and so fled to the Donatists, by whom he was rebaptized and made a deacon; this defection happened in the diocese of the bishop Valerius (?); so Augustin interposed through Maximius and Theodorus with Bishop Macrobius, but in vain. He deplores the disgrace done to the sacrament, as dishonor done to the sign of the King. The repetition is contradicted by the procedure with regard to the returning Maximianists. He corrects the misinterpretation of Ecclus. xxxiv. 30. He wishes for the Donatists the experience of the prodigal, that they may be forgiven by return to the Church and so attain to the profit of charity.

Great calamities were befalling the Church in all parts of the world. Victorianus, a presbyter, wrote to Augustin for relief from doubts as to the office of such afflictions; in the bishop's reply, [Ep. cxi.] possibly of Nov., 409, he mentions the cruelties of the Donatists at Hippo exceeding those of the Barbarians, especially in the resort to acidified lime, clubbing, robberies, and other destructive measures to compel rebaptism; forty-eight in one place were thus forced to a repetition. The coercion policy, in other words, had stimulated some of the Donatists to retaliation.

Donatus had resigned his proconsulship. Augustin writes [Ep.cxii.] at the end of 409 or beginning of 410 A.D., to express his regrets at not meeting him on his visit to Tibilis; his retirement would now give leisure for a larger development in graces, and would lead him to esteem the superiority of eternal things. He praises him for his official worth, which indeed was in everybody's mouth, but he urges him not to defer to that popularity, but to seek the higher approbation. After reminding him of the duty of Christian progress, he asks for a reply and an exhortation to be addressed to all his dependents at Sinitis and Hippo to return to the Church. Greetings are sent to his father, whom the son had been instrumental in converting to the faith.

Petilian of Constantina had written a treatise, de unico baptismo, which Constantinus had come into possession of through some Donatist presbyter, and then gave it to Augustin while they were in the country, imploring him to answer it. He did so, c. 410, in the book bearing the same title. He scorns those who desire secrecy in such matters; when the deeds are public let the discussion be. Petilian claims that the only true baptism is theirs: and therefore it is not repeated by the sacrilegious theorists. Yes, replies Augustin, baptism is indeed one, but it is Christ's, not yours; yours is only a repetition of the rite. We correct what is yours and recognize what is Christ's. Therefore we do not repeat it. So Christ corrected what was evil and recognized what was good among the Jews. So Paul exposed the sin of the heathen world but acknowledged what truth it had. Moreover you perform the ceremony, but it is to destruction: there is no real advantage in baptism outside of the Church. Petilian pleads for rebaptism because Paul rebaptized John's disciples; but, says Augustin, that is to declare John a heretic. These are two different things, as indeed Petilian himself suggests, some might say, and then gives two irrelevant passages, Matt. xii. 30, and vii. 21–23, as if the Catholics had no fellowship with Christ and were not recognized by Him. Augustin, after considering the import of these passages, avers the readiness of the Church to recognize the baptism of Christ as administered by Donatists when they return to the Church; for to deny Christ's baptism because it is administered by heretics, is to say Christ Himself should be denied, when even demons confess Him. There is a belief in God outside of the Church; the devils believe in Him outside of the Church. So there is one baptism of Christ which may exist also outside of the Church. Petilian's declaration that true baptism is where the true faith is, Augustin disproves by citing the case of the unbelieving and schismatic, yet baptized Corinthians. So all the ages of the kingdom bear witness to a like state of things. The action of Agrippinus and Cyprian on the one side, and of Stephen on the other, as to rebaptism is reviewed; differing in this, they yet maintained unity, especially Cyprian. Further, if the contact of evil men within the fellowship really defiles the good, then the Church perished in Cyprian's time; where could Donatus then have been spiritually born? If there is no such pollution, then there is no occasion to rage for separation. The origin of the schism is then denied from documentary testimony, and the charges declared to be not sustained; on the other hand, these archives prove the schismatics to have been traditors. A summary of the main points concludes his plea for the sole baptism as that of Christ. [Cp. Retractt. II. xxxiv.].

After this book against Petilian just mentioned had been finished, he wrote another work of larger proportions and with more thoroughness, in refutation of their schism, by the data of the Maximian schism, which he considered a full surrender of all their particularism. This has been styled: De Maximianistis contra Donatistas. It is lost, but noticed in the Retractations (II. xxxv.) immediately after de unico Baptismo.

At Carthage, about May 15, 411, he preached in praise of peace (Sermo ccclvii.). After its eulogy, he summons his hearers to the love of that peace; and recalls Donatists as alienated from the unity unto the concord which exists in the Church only. Patience and prayer are better means to their conquest than reproof. After the pentecostal fast he bade them exercise hospitality toward the guests who should attend the Conference.

The two edicts concerning the great Conference had been issued by Marcellinus. The Donatists had sent in their protest to the second, while the Catholic bishops sent in their acquiescence in a letter [Ep.cxxviii.], which is ascribed to Augustin's hand. It was of course written before June 1, 411, the day appointed for the opening. They agree to all the provisions for maintaining an orderly discussion; to the time and place of meeting; to the numbers to be present; to the requirement that all the delegated disputants sign their deliverances; to the countersignatures; to the order prohibiting the people from access to the Conference. If the Donatists prove the Church universal to have been lost and to be solely with them, the Catholic bishops will resign their sees; if, however, the collation prove the universality of the Church, then they suggest the recognition of the ordination and office of the Donatist clergy, and propose details for the succession in case of any jointure. The conciliatory example of Christ persuades them to this step; the peace of Christ in the Church is higher than the episcopate. The Donatist use of the civil authority against the Maximianists, and their gladness in receiving the returning schismatics without rebaptism, and without any diminution of their honors, give hope of a return to the root.

Before the meeting of the Conference, Augustin preached a sermon (No. ccclviii.) in Carthage, on peace and love, of which the main thoughts were the peace to which the Catholics cling and which they love under the persuasion of the divine testimonies; the victory of truth is love. He presents the Scripture proofs of charity and universality; the inheritance should not be divided. Donatus and Cæcilian were but men, but baptism is Christ's and not man's. The charity spread abroad in the heart is a broad commandment. He invites the Donatists to share in the Church's possessions, and to be bishops along with the Catholics, and pleads for a joint fraternal recognition; the Catholics seek peace and want to build up the Church. He finally requests the people to keep aloof from the place of dispute, but invokes their prayers in its behalf.

The objection to the second edict on the part of the Donatists respecting the restriction upon the number to be present at the collation, led the Catholics to write a second letter to Marcellinus, which is most likely also from the pen of Augustin. [Ep. cxxix.]. Solicitude over the opposition is expressed; some seem disposed to present a hindrance to the peaceful progress of the Conference; and yet the writers hope that the thought and suspicion may not prove true, but that the desire of the whole body may after all be to press into the unity of the Catholic Church. Then they go on, very wrongfully in such a document, to discuss their favorite note of the universality of the Church, as the body of Christ was not stolen, so neither are His members outside of the few in Africa, dead. From Jerusalem outward was to be its progress and thence it filled the whole world. The fact that the Donatists have the very same Scriptures as the Catholics which contain these proofs of universality, fills the complainants with grief for them. The Jews who denied the resurrection rejected also the New Testament; but the Donatists receive it, and yet they deny the note of universality, and accuse the Catholics of being traditors of the sacred books. Now at the collation probably they wish to be in full numbers, in order to search completely the Scriptures; and through their innumerable testimonies they long to come en masse, not to create a tumult, but to put an end to the old discord. It is true that they have found fault with our use of the State; and yet the Scriptures vindicate such a recourse, and the Donatists themselves appealed to Constantine. The Scriptures too show the mixed character of the Church, wheat and chaff, good and bad fish, to the final harvest, the winnowing, and the further shore. Perhaps they see the wrong of their opposition to the Church. The case of the Maximianists has shown their willingness to use the power of the State and to ignore rebaptism; and probably moved by these things, they want to come in such large numbers in the interest not of tumult but of peace. They desire to show that they are not so few as their enemies report them to be. The Catholic numbers exceed in proconsular Africa, and, except in Numidia, are more numerous than in the rest of the African provinces; and most of all when one comes to compare the whole world with the few Donatists. Why, however, could not the number be just as well certified by the subscription? Even though quiet be preserved, yet at such a Conference the murmur of such a crowd will impede the progress of the work. If they all can be present, the writers, nevertheless, will limit themselves to the delegation suggested by the Judge, and then no blame for disorder can attach to them. If, however, the protest has been made in behalf of unity, they all will be present joyfully to welcome the Donatists as brethren.

The Mandatum Catholicorum, a sort of voucher and letter of instruction for the disputants on the side of the State Church, was undoubtedly the product of Augustin's pen. After a preamble which attests the sufficiency of the Church through her divine proofs against all heretics and schismatics, and the desire of Church and State to settle the long pending controversy in Africa, and the duty to enlighten men as to the eternal salvation, which things had induced them to convene and to select defenders, there follows the note of the universality, which, as the great proposition, is expanded with many proof texts from the Old and the New Testament. This truth is to be defended against the Donatist assertion that the universal Church had perished through contamination with Cæcilian; for the Church is a mixed society of good and evil, and not to be condemned on this account, but its unity is to be preserved by toleration. If they maintain this view, the documents concerning Cæcilian's character must be examined. The contestants must prove that the Church was thus defiled, or else the evil do not defile the good in this unity. The mandate then gives Scriptural and also post-apostolic proofs on this point, especially from Cyprian, and quotes the Donatist action concerning the Maximianists. The next topic is baptism as a sacrament of Christ and not of man, and as independent of the character of the celebrant: the Maximian schism again affords material for the confutation of this Donatistic tenet. They are instructed also to use the archives to show that their opponents initiated civil appellation.

In the session of the second day, Augustin is the speaker, mainly on the matter of delay and adjournment.

In the third session, he appears as the chief disputant on the doctrinal and historical points, and also as answering the letter of the Donatists in reply to the mandate.

In a sermon preached after the close of the Conference, (Sermo ccclix. on Ecclus. xxv. 2), he exhorted all Christians to be brethren; the Catholics desire to have the Donatists unite with them in worship in the universal Church. The history of Cæcilian should not affect the doctrine of the body. He claims a triumph indeed for his side and rejoices over the many who are returning to the mother Church, but candidly confesses that many harden themselves in their opposition. His exordium appeals for a restoration of brotherly harmony.

A little later in the year, probably, Augustin preached from Gal. vi. 2–5(Sermo clxiv.), in which he rebukes those who say: "We are saints, we do not carry your burdens, therefore we do not communicate with you; "and says: "your ancestors carry burdens of separation, burdens of schism, burdens of heresy, burdens of dissension, burdens of animosity, burdens of false proofs, burdens of calumnious accusations." In your boast of non-participation in other's sins, you desert the flock, the threshing-floor and the net. The traditors who had condemned the absent Cæcilian dissolved connection with the whole world. He reminds them of the Maximianists; he charges them with breaking the parables, and yet inculcates patience. The whole sermon indicates that the effect of the conference had been to embitter both sides.

Another sermon (xcix.) on Luke vii. 36, 50, was also preached about this time, in which he conceives that the Puristic noli me tangeremay develop into a system for sin-pardoning, and justification and sanctification; the men of the Gesta Collationisare likely to bring about such a machine religion. Already do they say: if men do not remit sins, then what Christ says is false as to loosing on earth and in heaven. With this conception of the tendency of their tenets he further says against them, that the cleansing in baptism does not depend on the man.

In a fragment of another sermon (ccclx.), preached on the vigils of Maximian, he personates a Donatist, who has returned to the unity, thanking the Lord that the lost is found, and expressing his joy in the vine, the unity, the baptism and peace of Christ.

The authorized acts of the council of 411 were too unwieldy for either general or popular use, and a compendium framed from them was too obscure; so Augustin, about the close of 411, determined to make a digest, called the Breviculus collationis cum Donatistis. It gives the collations of the three days, but it is thoroughly disconnected without the official account, for too many links known to the actors alone are not apparent to the uninitiated; too much of what would throw light on the animus of the parties in power is passed over, and a considerable deal of the minor business necessary to the understanding of the spirit of the debate does not appear. A reader would certainly get a still more one-sided and intolerant idea of the Conference from the digest than from the Gesta. The analysis of the order of business would require a comparison with the Gesta Collationis, and that lies outside of our present purpose. [Cp. Retractt.II. xxxix.].

The decision of the Conference again stirred up a counter movement by the Circumcelliones, especially in Augustin's diocese, during which some terrible outrages were perpetrated; the presbyter Restitutus was killed; the presbyter Innocentius was clubbed and mutilated. A trial was instituted by Marcellinus and the crimes confessed. Augustin hastens to write to him [Ep.cxxxiii.], somewhere about the opening of 412 A.D., imploring that the punishment be not capital or retaliatory; restraint and labor would be just. He commends the tribune-notary's moderation in the examination, in that he did not resort to torture for extorting evidence, but only to whipping. He commands him, as bishop, not to proceed to extremity, which would be an injury to the Church, or at least to the diocese of Hippo. Since the pronouncing of the sentence presumably belonged to the proconsul, he had also indicted a letter to him.

Apringius, the proconsul, was a brother of Marcellinus. To him Augustin addressed a letter in the same interest, and at the same date. [Ep.cxxxiv.] For the use of his newly gained authority, he was accountable to God; he was also a Christian, so that Augustin felt a greater confidence in petitioning and in warning, and begs that he may regard his interference as a part of a bishop's zeal for the welfare of the Church. He repeats the story of the arrest of the Circumcelliones and Donatist clergy, the trial by Apringius's own brother, the tribunenotary, Marcellinus, and the gentleness of the hearing, in which the accused confessed their crime, especially as to the copresbyters. He now begs for a mild punishment; in the one case it cannot be strictly retaliatory; in that of the homicide he fears it may be capital punishment. Apringius must not only consider the State, but the Church, and respect her clemency. He is not only a ruler of exalted power but a son of Christian piety. Our enemies boast of persecution; we must give them no occasion for it. These acts should be read for the cure of the minds which have been perverted. If the extreme penalty has to fall, spare at least the children. He implores him to imitate the patience and mildness of the Church and of Christ.

Augustin, in 412, writes to Marcellinus [Ep. cxxxix.] expressing his delight that the proceedings connected with the trial are in preparation, and for the intention of having them read in the churches of the city, and, if possible, in all the churches of his diocese. The crimes mentioned are the same as before, with added confessions of many who were in some degree abettors. These are the men who refuse to commune with the Catholic Church for fear of pollution from wicked men, and yet refuse to leave a schism debased by such a fellowship. It was a question in Marcellinus's mind whether the Gestashould be read in the Donatist church of Theoprepia in Carthage. Augustin urges it, and if it be too small then in some other quarter, in that region of the city. Augustin pleads for a mild punishment in imitation of the clemency of the Church; however weak it may seem at the outset, men will afterward regard it with favor, and the reading of the Gesta will be more welcome and more effective by the contrast between Donatist cruelty and Catholic moderation. He speaks of the commission of the bishop Bonifacius and the bearer Peregrinus, who were empowered to treat upon some new measures for the benefit of the Church. The Donatist Bishop Macrobius was busy reopening the churches of his sect, followed by a band of both sexes. In the absence of Celer, a Donatist, his procurator, Spondeus, a Catholic, had broken their audacity. He is commended to the favorable notice of Marcellinus. While Spondeus was on a visit to Carthage, Macrobius had actually reopened the Donatist churches on the estates of Celer. He was assisted by Donatus, a rebaptized deacon and a leader in the slaughter; from which fact other outrages might be expected. Should the plea for mildness not be granted, Augustin asks that his letters urging clemency [Epp. cxxxiii. and cxxxiv.] be read along with the Gesta. At least let a remission be granted to give time for an appeal to the Emperors, for no martyrs desire their blood to be avenged by death. In apologizing for his inability to complete his work on the baptism of infants, he urges the variety of his labors; among other things he had completed the Breviculus Collationis, as a compend for those who had not the leisure to read the entire proceedings of the Conference; also a letter addressed to the Donatist laity.

The Donatists were charged with circulating the story of the bribery of the cognitor or judge of the Conference. The letter from the council of Zerta, June 14, 412, in refutation of this was written by Augustin, [Ep.cxli.] in which it is said that they had become acquainted with this rumor so easily credited by the common people. The vote of the council was to authorize a refutation of it as a falsehood. The Donatists had been convicted of mendacity in the charge which they had made and signed against the Catholics as traditors; they had also invented stories to account for the signature of an absent bishop. How can they be believed in such a charge against the cognitor? Since the acts of the Collation are so voluminous we present herewith a digest. The meeting, the election of disputants and scribes, the matter of the subscriptions, are then recapitulated. In the attempt at discussion, the whole aim of the Donatist disputants was to avoid coming to the point to be debated, while the Catholic representatives exerted themselves to reach just that goal and nothing else. When at last the Donatists were forced to the issue, they were vanquished by the clear testimony of the Scriptures to the universality of the Church. Anyone separated from this unity has not life; the wrath of God abides upon him. The communion with the wicked does not defile any one by the mere participation in the sacraments, but only by agreement with their deeds. All these truths they had to acknowledge. The Catholics had prevented a confusion between the doctrinal and historical sides of the question. In the discussion of the documents, the chief offset to all the points was found in the case of the Maximianists, although the Donatists plead that a case should not be prejudged by a case, nor a person by a person. All the accusations which had been concentrated against Cæcilian they were unable to meet with proofs. Defeated men are wont to suggest such a defense as the corruption of the judge. Then says the paper in effect: If you will believe us, let us hold fast to the unity which God commands and loves. But if you are unwilling to believe us, read the proceedings themselves, or allow them to be read to you, and do you yourselves test whether what we have written to you be true. If you decline all these, and will still cleave to the Donatists, we are clear from your judgment. If you will renounce the schism, we will welcome you to the peace of Christ, and you will have the profit of that sacrament which was administered among you to judgment.

The Donatist presbyters Saturninus and Eufrates had joined the Catholic Church and maintained their rank. Augustin writes [Ep.cxlii.], c. 412 A.D., to express his joy at their arrival and bids them not to grieve at his absence, for they are now in the one Church whose note of universality he expands as the one Body of the one Head, and as the one house in all the earth; in the unity of this house we rejoice as embracive of those transmarine churches, to whom the appeal had vainly been made by the Donatists. He who lives evilly in this Church eats and drinks condemnation to himself, but whoever lives correctly, another case and another person cannot prejudge him. The Donatists had protested against the parallel proofs drawn from the Maximianists, because a case should not be prejudged by a case nor a person by a person. On the Lord's threshing-floor the chaff must be tolerated. He exhorts them to a faithful discharge of their clerical duties, especially in mercifulness and also in prayer for the removal of the schism.

The hostility of the Donatists was increased by the Collation. Their clergy charged the judge with bribery, and protested against the unfairness of the trial, the compulsion of the meeting, the unjust decision. Augustin felt compelled to write, c. 412 A.D., to the people in order to stay the fury of their leaders. The treatise is known as Ad Donatistas post Collationem. Why make such a charge? Why does Primian say, it is unworthy for the sons of the martyrs to meet in the same place with the offspring of traditors? Why did they come? Why were they unable to prove the old accusations? And how are they the sons of martyrs? The universality of the Church was demonstrated at the Conference. Donatists do not commune with the churches addressed in those epistles which they read at their services, because they say these perished by communion with the African Cæcilians, and yet they put in the plea that a case should not be prejudged by a case nor a person by a person. He meets the Cæcilian charge by the Maximianists despite this caveat. He represents all the New Testament churches and the East as expostulating based on this very plea with the Donatists for separation from them. So, the case and the person of the bad does not prejudice the case and the person of the good; they must abide together until the end. He condemns their arrogant pretense to holiness. The wicked must be tolerated in the Church, but their deeds are not to be participated in. Cyprian would not destroy the unity because bad people were in it; frequent are the examples of such forbearance in the Scriptures, and the principle was not changed after the resurrection of Christ; it continued in force in the New Testament Church; the winnowing and severance come at the end of the world. They would perhaps deny their own words as uttered in the Conference were they not written; that was the beauty of requiring subscription. They charge too that the sentence against them was pronounced in the night. Augustin playfully speaks of many good things which have been said and done in the night. He subsequently reminds them of the days in which they tried to prove the origin of heresy, and their defeat at every point of the Cæcilian history. It appears here again that the Donatists had a considerable body of acts of their own. The plea of persecution as a note of the Church and as an experience of the Donatists was one of the points urged at the conference in the Donatist reply to the Catholic mandate, and by Primian, to which we have the usual answer. Another complaint of the Donatists was that they were tried by those who had been condemned by themselves, and were compelled to unite with sinners; to which Augustin gives a little Maximianist parallel and then considers the questions of purism, the paucity of believers, the need of discipline, the fellowship of a mixed community which ought not to degenerate into a participation in the deeds of the wicked therein. These are discussed with considerable detail of quotations from the Old and New Testaments. Some who thought Cæcilian guilty would not break the unity; they imitated Cyprian. He charges their clergy with duplicity. He reminds them of the deception practiced in presenting the signature of a Donatist, who was already dead; so with regard to the show of numbers in attendance and the alleged multitude absent, and also the means adopted for securing delay, the interruptions and turnings of the debate from the true object in view. He vindicates the cognitor's method and rulings. He then renews the discussion concerning the archival origin of the schism. In conclusion he addresses them as brethren and exhorts them to love peace and unity.

The Donatists of Cirta, clergy and people, had returned to the Catholic Church and had written a letter of thanks to Augustin for his preaching, under which they had been persuaded to renounce the schism. Augustin in reply [Ep. cxliv.], probably at end of 412 A.D., says that this is not man's work, but God's. Their allusion to the conversion of the drunken and luxurious Polemo by Xenocrates, draws from him the reflection, that such a change of character, though not a Christian repentance, is, nevertheless, a work of God. So, he bids them not to give thanks to himself but to God, for their return to the unity. Those who still are alienated, whether from love or fear, he charges to remember the undeceived scrutiny of God; to weigh Scripture testimony as to the universality of the Church; and the documents as to the origin of the schism. The case has been tried or not been tried by the transmarine churches; if not, then there is no existing ground for the separation; if it has, the defeated ones are the separatists. But alas! the obstacles to their persuasion are well-nigh insuperable. He hopes that the mutual desire for his visit to them may be fulfilled.

About the beginning of the year 413, appeared the book De Fide et Operibus. In Chap. iv. 6, he speaks of the need of coercion against the Donatists as disturbers of the peace of the Church, as separaters of the tares from the wheat before the time, as those who have blindly preferred to cut themselves off from the unity; commixture of evil and good is a necessity, and we ought to remain in that fellowship which is not at all destitute of discipline. [Cp. Retractt. II. xxxviii.]

Donatus, a Donatist presbyter, and another person connected with that body, had been arrested by order of Augustin about the beginning of 416 A.D. Mounted upon a beast against his will, he dashed himself to the ground and so received injuries which his less obstinate companion escaped. Augustin writes [Ep.clxxiii.] to vindicate himself as concerned about the salvation of the recusants, and puts the blame of the wounds upon the offender. Donatus urged in opposition to this style of conversion that no one should be compelled to be good. Augustin claims on the other hand that many are compelled to take the good office of a bishop against their will. Donatus argues that God had given us free will, therefore a man should not be compelled even to be good. Augustin replies that the effort of a good will is to restrain and change the evil will, because of the awful results which follow a vitiated will. Why were the Israelites compelled to go to the land of promise? Why was Paul forced to turn from persecution to the embrace of the truth? Why do parents correct children? Why are negligent shepherds blamed? You are an errant sheep, with the Lord's mark upon you, and I as shepherd must save you from perishing. Of your own will you threw yourself into a well, but it would have been wicked to leave you there where you had cast yourself according to your will, and hence the attendants took you out; how much more is it a duty to save you from eternal death. Besides, it is unlawful to inflict death upon yourself. He reminds him that the Scriptures do not allow suicide; and controverts his use of I. Cor. xiii. 3, "though I give my body to be burned." Severed from charity and unity, nothing can profit, not even the surrender of the body to burning. The points of the recent joint Conference are then dwelt upon. Donatus was understood to have criticized the saying of his party as to the Maximianist parallel: do not prejudge a case by a case or a person by a person. Augustin twits him in this wise: If you object to this, then you are deceived concerning it, because you oppose your authority to theirs, and if you say it is not true, the hope of vindicating the great schism falls through entirely. He presses him to weigh all the proceedings. But Donatus objects also that the Lord did not cause the seventy to come back, and did not put a barrier in the way of the twelve when he asked, "Will ye also go away?" Augustin says that was in the beginning of Christianity; kings were not yet converted; now the State helps the Church. Our Lord said prophetically, Compel them to come in. So we hunt you in the hedges; the unwilling sheep is brought to the true pasture.

The series of Tractatus on the Gospel of John, which are ascribed to 416 A.D., contain many reflections on Donatism. We can only notice the passages:

       Tractatus IV.   in Jo. i. 19–33.
       Tractatus V.   in Jo. i. 33.
       Tractatus VI.   in Jo. i. 32, 33. Quite fully.
       Tractatus IX.   in Jo. ii. 1–11.
       Tractatus X.   in Jo. ii. 12–21.
       Tractatus XI.   in Jo. ii. 23–25, and iii. 1–5.
       Tractatus XII. in Jo. iii. 6–21.

Tractatus XIII. in Jo. iii. 22–29.

To the same year are ascribed the Tractatus on the I. Ep.of John.

Tractatus I.	1 Jo. i.and ii. 1–11.
Tractatus II.	1 Jo. ii. 12–17.
Tractatus III.	1 Jo. ii. 18–27.
Tractatus IV.	1 Jo. iii. 1–8.

In the Retractations, II. xlvi., we read of a book addressed to Emeritus, the Donatist bishop of Cæsarea, in the province of Mauritania Cæsariensis. [See Ep.lxxxvii.] He speaks of him as the best of the seven Donatist disputants at the Conference. The work marked briefly the lines on which the Donatists were defeated. Its title is: Ad Emeritum Donatistarum Episcopum, post collationem, liber unus. Since the Retractations place it before De Gestis Pelagii, and De Correctione Donatistarum, it was most likely written in the beginning of 417 A.D.

Boniface had requested from Augustin a letter of instructions on the relation of the Donatists to the Arians. The bishop replies, c. 417 [Ep. clxxxv.], which he himself calls a book de Correctione Donatistarum. [Cp. Retractt. II. xlviii.]. Since this is translated in the present volume, we will omit any further notice.

The above-mentioned Emeritus was present at a Synod of the Catholics, near Deuterius, September 20, 418. At a service held two days after, Augustin preached the Sermo ad Cæsariensis Ecclesiæ plebem. Emeritus was present. In the church during a previous colloquy with Augustin he had said: I cannot will what you will, but I can will what I will. Augustin in this sermon (and the writing has all the abruptness and repetition of an extempore address) urges him to will what God wills, viz., peace, and that now, in response to the cry of the people; and if you ask why I, who call you schismatics and heretics, desire to receive you, it is because you are brethren; because you have the baptism of Christ; because I want you to have salvation: one can have everything outside the Church except salvation; he can have honor, he can have the sacraments, he can sing Allelulia, he can respond Amen, he can hold to the gospels, he can have faith in the name of the Father and the Son and the Holy Spirit, and can preach. Persecution after all is rather of you. The failure of the archival evidence as to Cæcilian is alleged as usual, and hence no reason for separation exists. He recites too the story of the seizure, escape, reseizure, compulsory baptism and ordination of Petilian, while at the time a Catholic catechumen. This occurred at Constantina, when that city and region were largely Donatist. He was seized unto death, do we not draw him to salvation? Here or nowhere, says Augustin, repeating the voice of the people, is the place for peace.

There was a gathering of clergy (the bishops Alypius, Augustinus, Possidius, Rusticus Palladius, etc., many presbyters and deacons and a considerable number of people) in the exedra of the larger church at Cæsarea, c. 418 A.D. Emeritus, the Donatist bishop of the city, was also present. Augustin addresses those devoted to the unity, and says that when he came to the city on the day before yesterday he found Emeritus returned from a journey. Augustin met him in the street and invited him to the Church, and Emeritus consented without any demur. The sermon of Augustin is full of the peace, love and related themes of the Church, in hope of winning Emeritus. He alludes to the many conversions in the city and since the collation; if Emeritus has anything new to say in defense of his side, he invites him to state it. Emeritus had been reported as affirming that at the Conference the Donatists were overcome by power rather than by truth. Augustin then addresses inquiries to Emeritus directly: as to why he had come if he was defeated at the council; or if he thought his party had triumphed, then to state the ground for such an opinion. Emeritus said: The acts show whether I am defeated or not, whether I am defeated by truth or oppressed by power. Augustin: Then why do you come? Emeritus: That I might say this very thing which you ask, and so on. Under some taunting and arrogant observations to the brethren, Emeritus keeps quiet. From Augustin's statement it appears that the Acts were read during Lent, at Thagaste, Constantina, Hippo, and all the faithful churches. Part of these Gesta are then read by Alypius, viz, the imperial convocation of the Conference, and comments are made by Augustin. Then follows his application of the lessons afforded by the Maximianist schism, in which he says the Donatists make shipwreck of all their tenets. Emeritus, however, remained a silent hearer. The account of the above meeting is given in the treatise: De Gestis cum Emerito, Cæsariensi Donatistarum Episcopo liber unus. [Cp. Retractt. II. li.]

The book de Patientiais assigned to 418 A.D. In Chapter xiii. he contrasts genuine and false martyrdom.

Dulcitius had been appointed Tribune-notary. The effect of his carrying out of the renewed edicts against the Donatists was signalized by many conversions, but also by many suicides. He had written to Augustin requesting directions about how he ought to proceed against the heretics. Augustin replies [Ep.cciv.], c. 420 A.D., that his work had indeed persuaded many to return to their salvation, but others were stirred either to kill the Catholics or themselves. We indeed do desire the return of all to unity, yet some are doubtless predestinated to perish by an occult yet just decree of God. They perish not only in their own fires but in that of Gehenna. The Church grieves over them as David over his son, although they have met the deserved punishment of rebels. Augustin does not find fault with the notary's edict at Thamugada, only with the phrase: You may know that you are to be given over to the death which you deserve; for that is not contained in the rescripts. In the second edict there is a clearer statement of the notary's aim. Augustin also criticizes his courtesy toward Gaudentius, the Donatist bishop of Thamugada. As to a special reply to that bishop Augustin urges a more diligent refutation of the fallacious doctrines by which the Donatists are accustomed to be seduced. He had already done this in very many works, but adds some points by way of suggestion. He alone is a martyr who dies for a true cause. Man's will is free, but nevertheless amenable to divine and human laws. The State can punish not only adulteries and homicides, but also sacrileges. Many think it strange that we do not rebaptize, but the sacrament once given ought not to be repeated. Suicides are utterly prohibited by the Scriptures. The case of Razius gives the Donatist no pretext, for the deed is simply mentioned but not commended. (II. Mac. xiv. 37–46). In conclusion he intimates that in answer to the united wish of the people of Thamugada, of himself and of Eleusinus, the tribune of that place, that Augustin should answer both epistles of

Gaudentius, the Donatist bishop, and especially the latter of the two, which contained Scriptural proofs, he will write such a criticism.

Dulcitius had written a pacific letter to Gaudentius, the Donatist bishop of Thamugada, one of the quieter members of the seven Donatist disputants, concerning the enforcement of the imperial edicts. Gaudentius replied in two epistles, one short, the other longer and fortified by Scripture proofs. Augustin was requested to answer these, which he does (c. 420) in the work Contra Gaudentium Donatistarum Episcopum, Libra duo. In Book I. he makes a change of form from the Petilian cast of personal dialogue, because of the captious fault found with that way as savoring of untruth, and takes a duller formula, "Verba Epistolæ" and "ad hæc responsio," whose dryness and literality the most sensitive Donatist could take no exception to. In the first epistle of Gaudentius, the fairly courteous strain in which he had replied to the tribune-notary, with titles and recognition of character, Augustin rather resents by saying that the Catholic had treated the heretic too kindly and incautiously, and bids Gaudentius consider what he had said at the Collation. Gaudentius proposes to remain in the communion where the name of God and of his Christ is and where the Sacraments are, and pleads for religious liberty against compulsion as to matters of faith; and concludes, by another hand, with wishing him well and desiring his recession from the disquieting of Christians. Augustin objects that Gaudentius had not reproduced the language of Dulcitius correctly, and accuses the Donatists of holding the truth of baptism in the iniquity of human error; he comments on their false eagerness for death; he responds to all the good wishes for the tribune, but not that he should cease from correcting the heretics.

The second epistle of Gaudentius is mainly a protest from Scriptural grounds; against persecution he brings forward the case of Gabinus, who, if bad, should not have been received without correction, that is, baptism; but if innocent, why kill the innocent Donatists from whom he came to you? The false rumor about Emeritus, as having turned Catholic, is another instance of this persecution. The duty of a persecuted pastor is to be a doer of the law and to lay down his life for the sheep; there is no place whither the persecuted may now flee; the divine right of free will is restrained by the arbitrary laws of the emperor; persecution is a note of the Church from the blessings attached to it by Christ and the apostles. The peace of Christ invites the willing but does not compel the unwilling; a thing very different from the war-bearing peace and the bloody unity which their oppressors present. We rejoice in the hatred of the world; there is a martyr host of the apocalypse; Christians may yield up their souls in testimony against sacrilege, as Razius did. He begs Dulcitius to turn to the few who have the solidity and not the semblance of truth. God gave prophets not kings to teach the people: the Savior sent fishermen not soldiers. God never needs the aid of soldiers. Gaudentius charges the Catholics with coveting the Donatist possessions. The farewell is in another handwriting, in which he wishes Dulcitius well, and advises him to pursue a lenient and temperate course.

The points of Augustin's reply are in no way different save form from those so constantly presented, unless there be an increase of roughness and a more hardened idea of the Church's right to use coercion. As to Gabinus, the Church's course regarding him is a vindication of the right to receive a convert without rebaptism: in communion with charity and unity he received the profit of that rite which had been administered among the Donatists. In the case of Emeritus, Augustin confesses that the rumor of his having turned Catholic was false; but Emeritus came to Cæsarea of his own will; he came to the Church where a multitude was present; he could say nothing for his or his party's defense; he kept quiet. The argument against suicide from the case of Razius is well made; he died rather in suffering for the state; and besides the narrative does not commend the deed, but only states it; then too the books have not the weight that the Law, the Prophets and the Psalms carry with them. The plea for correction is precisely as usual. The doctrines of universality and unity and charity are incidentally brought forward. Circumcelliones, Secundus and Maximianists furnish the concluding parallels.

Book II. Gaudentius had written a reply to Augustin's first book. He had taken refuge under the example of Cyprian; but Augustin now refers him to the writings of Cyprian on De Simplicitate Prælatorum seu De Catholicæ Ecclesiæ unitate, showing Cyprian's belief in the universality of the Church which Augustin expands by the explanation of the term Catholic. Purgation of the Church is not by separation, but by toleration, as Cyprian too held in his letter to Maximus and others. The explanation of the field not as the Church, but rather as the world outside of the Church, had been supported at the Conference and is repeated by Gaudentius; and also its alternative, that were the field the Church then it must have perished from the tares which were in it. If so, says Augustin, then the ancestors of the Donatists would have perished. The period of separation is at the end, when the Gospel shall have been preached in the whole world. As to their theme of rebaptism, Augustin replies that he had already before referred him to his Maximianist practice, so that the action of Agrippinus and Cyprian are vain for him. And then too, according to Cyprian's own confession, and Stephen's testimony, there were crimes in the Church in their day; did the Church perish then? If so where was Donatus born? If not, then why did the party of Donatus separate? They are guilty of the very schism which Cyprian particularly deprecated as a cure, instead of toleration and discipline, for the ills of the Church. As to baptism: The Catholics recognize the Donatist rite, for the sacrament cannot be lost upon those who receive it among Catholics and then pass over to heretics; they have the truth but in iniquity; the truth is not the property of the Donatists. The apostle recognized such truth as he found among the Gentiles. Gaudentius had vindicated his reference to the tribune's letter, as to the Donatists having the names of God and of his Christ, and quoted the passage in proof. Augustin acknowledges his mistake, which, however, was not intentional, and he apologizes for the tribune's error as that of a military man who was not familiar with theology. Since Gaudentius had called the tribune religious in his first letter, Augustin accuses him of insincerity and berates him as superstitious. He also corrects Gaudentius for saying that God sent Jonah not to the king but only to the people of Nineveh, for the king compelled the humiliation of his subjects. In conclusion he quotes from Cyprian's letter to Maximus in behalf of universality and tolerant unity. His exordium is an earnest appeal to the Catholics to maintain all the notes of the Church. [Cp. Retractt. II. lix.].

Felicia had been a Donatist originally and was converted by force. She had devoted herself to the virgin life and apparently had become head of a religious house; but because of some wicked deeds of the clergy, possibly the extortion and rapacity of Antonius at Fussala, she was much disturbed and seemed inclined to relapse into her earlier puristic notions, if not to return to the body that upheld them. To quiet her doubts Augustin writes Ep. ccviii. c. 423. The Lord had predicted offenses. There are two kinds of shepherds over the flock, and will be to the end: the flock too has the good and the bad in it. The gathering is the present duty, the separation will be the future one; this latter is the Lord's prerogative. To abide in unity under such circumstances is a duty until the winnowing, and one is to believe what these shepherds teach, not what they do. Good and bad are therefore in the world under the widely diffused Catholic Church; the Donatist has no such note of universality. Love Christ and the Church, and then He will not permit you to lose the fruit of your virginity and to perish with the lost. If you go out of this life, separated from the unity of the body of Christ, this preserved integrity of the body will not profit you. You were compelled to come in; be thankful to those who compelled you. Show your devotion to the Lord, as your only hope, by being unmoved with these offenses, and by cleaving to his body, the Church.

A letter addressed to Pope Cœlestine is ascribed to Augustin [Ep.ccix. c. 423]; its authenticity has been disputed. The author, in giving an account of the appointment of Antonius as bishop of Fussala, remarks that at Fussala, a castellum about forty miles distant from Hippo, as in all the adjoining region, there had been a

Donatist population; in Fussala itself there had not been a solitary Catholic; the Punic was the common language. The coercive measures had converted the whole territory, but the process had also aroused a violent opposition in the form of robbery, beating, blinding, murder. After its conversion, the distance from Hippo and the great numbers to be instructed, required a new bishopric, the history of which and the troubles growing out of it, the author further relates.

In that valuable book De doctrina christiana, (begun in 397, but ended in 426, including the part having reference to our subject III. xxx. 42), Augustin quotes approvingly from the book of Tychonius the De septem regulis, and prefaces a discussion of these rules by an allusion to the treatise of Tychonius, which had refuted some of the narrow and puristic doctrines of the Church, as held by his own party; this we have already seen was answered by Parmenian, whose letter in turn was dissected by Augustin. The first, second, fourth and seventh of these rules bear especially upon the doctrinal points under discussion. [Cp. Retractt. II. iv. and Tychonius de Septem Regulisis reprinted in Migne. Pat. Lat. xviii.]

In his de Hœresibus [c. 428 A.D.] Chapter lxix. gives a brief account of the Donatiani or Donatistæ: (a) as to origin and progress; (b) Donatus's view of the Trinity; (c) the Montenses at Rome; (d) the Circumcelliones; (e) the schism of Maximian.

This was his parting arrow after the thirty-six years of battle. Catholics and Donatists passed under the persecutions of the Arian Vandals. Two years after this treatise Augustin laid aside his weapons to enter the land of eternal peace and unity.

More or less extended allusions are made to Donatism in the following sermons, arranged in the order of the Benedictine editions; for the years in which they were delivered cannot be determined. Want of space prevents the presentation of any analysis.

Sermo X.	1 Kings iii. 16–28.
Sermo XLV.	Is. lvii. 13 and 2 Cor. vii. 1.
Sermo XLVI.	Ez. xxxiv. 1–16.
Sermo XLVII.	Ez. xxxiv. 17–31.
Sermo LXXI.	Matt. xii. 32.
Sermo LXXXVIII.	Matt. xx. 30–34.
404	
Sermo XC.	Matt. xxii. 1–14.
Sermo CVII.	Luc. xii. 13–21.
Sermo CXXIX.	Jo. v. 39–47.
Sermo CXXXVII.	Jo. x. 1–16.
Sermo CXXXVIII.	Jo. x. 11–16.
Sermo CLXXXIII.	1 Jo. iv. 2.
Sermo CCXVIII.	Luc. xxiv. 38–47.
Sermo CCXLIX.	Jo. xxi. 1–14.
Sermo CCLII.	Jo. xxi. 1–14.
Sermo CCLXV.	The Ascension.
Sermo CCLXVI.	Ps. cxli.(cxl.) 5.
Sermo CCLXVIII.	Pentecost.
Sermo CCLXIX.	Pentecost.

Sermo CCLXXXV. Anniversary of the martyrs Castus and Æmilus.
Sermo CCXCII. John the Baptist.
Sermo CCCXXV. Anniversary of the Twenty Martyrs.

Similar references are to be found in the

expositions and sermons based on the Psalms. The first column is the Hebrew and English order; the second that of LXX. and Vulgate.

Exposition of Psalms XI. (X.)
Exposition of Psalms XXVI. (XXV.) Sermon.
Exposition of Psalms XXXI. (XXX.) Sermons I. and II. Exposition of Psalms XXXIII. (XXXII.) Sermon II.
Exposition of Psalms XXXIV. (XXXIII.) Sermon II.
Exposition of Psalms XXXVI. (XXXV.) Sermon.
Exposition of Psalms XXXVII. (XXXVI.) Sermons II. (archival) and III.
Exposition of Psalms XL. (XXXIX.) Sermon.
Exposition of Psalms LV. (LIV.) Sermon.
Exposition of Psalms LVIII. (LVII.) Sermon.
Exposition of Psalms LXXXVI. (LXXXV.) Sermon.
Exposition of Psalms XCIX. (XCVIII.) Sermon.
Exposition of Psalms CXX. (CXIX.) Sermon.
Exposition of Psalms CXXV. (CXXIV.) Sermon.
Exposition of Psalms CXXXIII. (CXXXII.) Sermon.
Exposition of Psalms CXLVI. (CXLV.) Sermon.
Exposition of Psalms CXLVII. 12–20 (CXLVII.) Sermon.
Exposition of Psalms CXLIX. Sermon.

The time of writing the de Utilitate Jejuniis unknown. Chapter V. 9, contrasts pagan, heretical and Catholic fasts; heretics claim indeed to fast in order to please God; how can they, when they sever the unity? All heretics perish; they are the dividers of the inheritance of Christ. ⎯⎯⎯⎯⎯⎯⎯⎯⎯

In conclusion the reviser desires to commend the fidelity and lucidity of the translation made by the Rev. J. R. King, M.A.

No changes made by the reviser have been indicated, since all could not be without confusion. The translation had taken most of its notes and references from the Benedictines. The citations of Cyprian are according to the numerals in Hartel's edition.

www.ingramcontent.com/pod-product-compliance
Lightning Source LLC
Chambersburg PA
CBHW052047070526
44584CB00018B/2642